MW01519587

CONTENTS.

—❊—

	Page.
The Reptile Army, Part I.	1
The same, Part II.	10
The Insect Army	20
The Departure of Israel	29
The Giving of the Law, Part I.	38
The same, Part II.	48
More about Job, Part I.	60
The same, Part II.	67
The same, Part III.	74
The King and the False Prophet, Part I.	80
The same, Part II.	89
The same, Part III.	99
Rahab and the Spies	105
Jericho	111
The Praying Youth	119
The Ark and Dagon	125
The Child of David	134
Obadiah	140

CONTENTS.

	Page.
Elijah, and the false Prophets	148
The Prayer of Elijah	156
The little Cloud	162
The Flight of Elijah	170
The Lord's Interview with Elijah on Mount Horeb	176
The Call of Elisha	182
The Widow's Pot of Oil	189
The Shunemite's Son	197
The Vision of Isaiah	204
The Enquiry of Peter	210
The Saviour's Charge	215
The Lame Man Healed	221
The Gift of Tongues	228
Cornelius, Part I.	235
Cornelius, Part II.	240
The Departure of Paul	246

THE REPTILE ARMY,

STORY I.

THE REPTILE ARMY.

PART I.

PHARAOH was a proud and wicked king of Egypt; he held the people of Israel in cruel bondage, and would not set them free, though God bade him.

And his subjects were as cruel as he was. So God, to show that he was angry with them, turned the fine river Nile, which ran through the land, into blood.[1] And, as they were all very fond of the water, this was a great trouble; still they would not obey God's command. How hard is the human heart, and how many strokes will it bear, without being the better. It is so hard, that no one but God can soften it. O that he would give me his Spirit, to make mine humble and contrite.[2]

And the Lord sent to Pharaoh again to charge him to set his people free. They did not belong to the king of Egypt, and he had no right to make them slaves, or to keep them in bondage; they were the Lord's. And am I not? And is not every one the Lord's? Yes, for he made, and he preserves, and blesses every one, and at every moment. No one could live, if God did not hold him up in life. Every one, therefore, and at all times, should love and serve him.[3]

But why did God send again to Pharaoh? why did he not at once cut him down? Because he is very patient, and bears long even with the wicked; and because he does not desire the death of a sinner, but rather that he would turn to God, and seek for his mercy.[4] And if he be so kind to those who will not obey his will, will he not be much more so, to those who pray for his favour, and who indeed desire to love and serve him? We are sure that he will.

The Lord charged Moses to tell Pharaoh, that, if he would not obey his voice, he would bid so many frogs come up on every part of the land, as should be a great plague both to him and his subjects. But he did not care about the message which God sent him. Perhaps the people in his palace said, that no one need be afraid of frogs; that they could readily drive them away, or kill them; or that the threatening could not be fulfilled, as so many frogs, as would fill the kingdom, did not exist; and, of course, that no one could bring them all together into Egypt. And so they did not mind God's warning. Wicked people now do not care about God's warnings.

God never punished any one without good reason, or without warning him. He sent Noah to warn the old world; and that good man did so for one hundred and twenty years. And the Lord Jesus came himself, and warned Jerusalem, and wept over it. And who have not been warned to avoid what is wrong, to seek after the favour of God, and the pardon of their sins for Christ's sake? Have you not been thus warned, by conscience, by the Bible, by parents, and ministers, and perhaps by dying friends ?⁵   And have we minded what they have said ?

God said, that he would punish Pharaoh and his people by bringing up frogs on all the land.   But why did he not send lions and bears to tear them in pieces, or an angel to cut them off?   He could have done this as easily as he brought up an army of reptiles; but he did not.   Perhaps it was to mortify the pride of Pharaoh; to show him, that God could humble him to the dust even by frogs. He can bring down the highest who dare to oppose him, and by a fly, or a frog, or a worm.   Herod, at his bidding, was eaten up of worms.⁶

And now, God bade Aaron stretch out his rod over the streams and rivers, and ponds of Egypt, and the frogs knew that they were called for, and they came up, and covered the land.   The unbelief of Pharaoh and his courtiers, did not prevent God's word from being fulfilled.   The heavens and the earth may pass away, sooner than any word of God can fail.⁷   All creatures are at his control; they listen to his voice, and obey it.   When God gave the word, the fiery flying serpents came into the camp of Israel, and bit the people. Yea, the very earth opened its mouth, when he told it to do so, and swallowed up Korah and his company. The creatures change even their nature at the command of their Creator. Thus the fire would not burn the three children. And thus the ravens did not rob Elijah of his food, as we might readily have supposed, but they brought him " bread and flesh in the morning, and again in the evening." And so, the viper would not bite and sting Paul; nor would the lions eat up Daniel, though he was cast into their den. Surely, then, if God be our friend, we need not fear any thing.

But why did Aaron stretch out the rod which was in his hand? Could not God have brought up the frogs without it? No doubt he could. But it is his will that we should use the means which he appoints. He could have healed Hezekiah, in answer to his prayer, in an instant, but he did not choose to do so; and what he chooses is best. He bade the prophet Isaiah tell him to put figs on his wound, and he would be healed. He could have cured Naaman at once, but it was his will, that he should go and wash himself in Jordan seven times. He could give us harvests without any labour ; but he does not do so, unless men plough and sow their fields ; yet though the means must be used, he alone can bless and make them useful. And so it is as to spiritual blessings ; we must think, and read the Bible, and pray, and go to the house of God to hear his holy word.[8] It is in this way alone that God has promised to meet with us, and to do us good.

And the frogs, at the call of God, crept out of the ponds, and lakes, and rivers, and came, leaping from every quarter, into all the villages, towns, and cities. There was not one in which they did not abound. They came by hundreds, and thousands, and millions, and millions of millions. They were so many, that they could no more be numbered than the sand on the sea shore. Every cottage, storehouse, and mansion, and even the palace of the king, was full of them. No one could look any where without seeing them ; or walk any where without stepping on them.　They even got up into all the rooms of the houses; and they came in again faster than they could be driven out; so the people could not find a place where they were not.

No one can flee away from God's judgments. He can send, and seek out, and punish his foes, wherever they may be.[9]　The voice of God found out Adam and Eve, and made them come forth, though they were hid among the thick leaves of the trees of Paradise.　Jonah went down into the hold of a ship, to get away from God and his duty, but God bade a great wind go after him, and compel him to do what he told him.[10]

It is true of every one of us, that we have not obeyed his holy commands.　Each one, and that too many times, has deserved his anger.　There is no place where we can hide ourselves from his all-seeing eyes.　We " cannot go from his Spirit, or flee from his presence."　Therefore let us not be so foolish as to try to do so.　Rather let us go to his throne of grace to confess our sins, and ask him, for Jesus' sake, to pardon and save us.[11]　If we do so, we are sure that he will hear our prayer, and become our friend and father. Then we should be safe and happy in the pathless desert, or on the stormy ocean; then, without any fear, we may walk through " the valley of the shadow of death." [12] And when the wicked at that great day shall "call for the rocks to fall on them, and the hills to cover them," and hide them from the frowns of the Judge, his pardoned children shall lift up their eyes with a joy that is " unspeakable, and full of glory !" [13]

QUESTIONS.

1. Into what did God turn the waters of the river Nile?

2. For what should we pray, that our hearts may be humble and contrite?

3. As we are the Lord's, what should we do at all times?

4. What does God rather desire than the death of a sinner?

5. How have we been warned to seek after God's favour, and the pardon of our sins?

6. How did God punish Herod?

7. What may pass away sooner than any word of God can fail?

8. How may we expect God to bless us with spiritual blessngs?

9. What can God do?

10. How did God compel Jonah to do what he told him?

11. What should we rather do than try to hide ourselves from God?

12. Where may we be safe and happy, if God be our friend?

13. When the wicked call for the rocks to fall on them, to hide them from their Judge, what will his pardoned servants then do?

STORY II.

—✿—

THE REPTILE ARMY.

You have.heard how the great army of frogs came up at God's bidding, and filled all the land of Egypt; and every house, and the palace of the king; and there was no place where they were not.

This was a dreadful state of things, for the people had no rest night or day. These filthy creatures leaped up on their very beds, and crawled over them. No doubt, but that the people were awake, a long while, as long as they could keep their eyes open.

What a mercy it is to be kept in safety, and to enjoy sweet sleep through the night. Wearisome nights were appointed to Job; and so they are to many. How thankful we should be if we lie down, night after night, and sleep, and rise again in peace and comfort![1] How earnestly should we pray God to bless, and to have mercy on those who cannot do so! And how thankfully should we say, " I laid down, and slept, and rose again, for the Lord sustained me. I will bless the Lord at all times; morning and evening, and at noonday, I will call upon him. His praise shall be continually on my lips!"[2] And do we do so?

But why did not God send the frogs to plague Pharaoh alone, as he was chiefly to blame? Why did he send them to annoy his subjects? No doubt, because they, as well as their king, were the foes of Israel. If we take part in the bad conduct of any one, or approve of it, we shall share in what they suffer for their sins.[3]

But the frogs came up into "the ovens" of the people of Egypt. How could they get into their ovens?[4] Why, their ovens were not like ours; for they made holes in the ground, in the sides of which were tiles; these were heated, and the cakes stuck on them, and baked.' Now, though frogs could not very well get up into our ovens, they would readily fill up such ovens as these; and they did so; and the people knew not how to bake their bread.

The reptiles got even into the vessels in which the dough was made, and were mixed up with it. It would be a great trial to any of us to eat of such bread. Let us thank God, that he feeds us every day "with the finest of the wheat."⁶

God can punish those who will not mind what he says to them, in very many ways. They may plant or sow the ground, but he may bid the earth not yield its fruit. Or if the seed should spring up, he may speak to the rain, and it will hear his voice, and it may drown the blade; or he can command his sun to scorch or burn it; and even if we should reap the precious grain, and make it into bread, the bread would not do us any good, without God's blessing.'

How earnestly, then, should we ask him to give us his blessing; and not eat our food, as too many do, like the horse, or the sheep, or the cow.' We are told, in the book of Samuel, that the people would not eat, till the Prophet had prayed for a blessing. When Paul was on his voyage to Rome, before he broke the bread for the people in the ship, he gave thanks. And the Lord Jesus always did so, before he fed the multitude.* If we do not give thanks, and ask his blessing, we shall have something in our bread much worse than a frog; for he will send his curse on the very blessings which we enjoy,' Mal. ii. 2.

When Pharaoh beheld these loathsome reptiles all around, and in his palace, and heard them croaking in every room; when he saw them in the dishes on his table, and felt them crawling over him on his bed, no doubt he was in a great rage. Perhaps he was angry with his servants,—and bade them sweep out the frogs; but they could not do it; for, as fast as they did so, they came in again. With all their pains, they could not help their

---

* 1 Sam. ix. 13; Acts xxvii. 35; Matth. xv. 36.

master. In all our troubles, we must say, as the king did to the woman at the siege of Samaria, " If God do not help, how can I help ?"[10]

We should trust in God, and not in creatures, or in vain idols, if we would be happy. The foes of Israel trusted in the big giant Goliath; but a mere lad, by God's help, with a sling and a stone, brought him to the ground. They relied on their idol god Dagon; but the Lord smote him, and he fell from the place where they set him up, and his hands and his feet were broken to pieces. God has said, " Cursed is the man that trusteth in man, and maketh flesh his arm, and whose heart departeth from the Lord,"[11] Jer. xvii. 5. And so Pharaoh found it; for he trusted in his chariots, and horses, in his men of war, and in his idol gods; and an army of frogs,—little creatures which can neither sting nor bite,—subdued him. " It is a fearful thing to fall into the hands of the living God."[12]

And Pharaoh could not live any longer among these hateful reptiles; so he called for Moses, and said, " Intreat the Lord, that he may take away the frogs from me, and from my people; and I will let the people go, that they may sacrifice unto the Lord." Persons who, when they are in health, despise the servants of the Lord, send for them, and are glad to have their visits, and their prayers, when they are afflicted or dying. When the rich man was in hell, he wanted Lazarus, to whom, when on earth, he would not give the crumbs which fell from his table, to come to his help, to bring a " drop of water to cool his parched tongue." [13]

Moses did not say, Pray for yourself; for I will not be troubled about you any more. As you would not obey God's word, you must bear his frown, and his judgments. No; but he said, Well, I will do so; appoint a time, and I will pray God, that the frogs may be killed, or removed from thee, and from thy subjects, and that they may remain in the river only; that you may know, that none but God can do it; and that he alone can hear and answer prayer.

Pharaoh did not ask Moses to pray for him that his sins might be forgiven, but only that the frogs, which made him and his people so wretched, might be taken away. Wicked people are often more troubled about the sorrows their sins bring on them, than the pardon of their guilt. Cain said, I shall be a vagabond on the face of the earth; and people, wherever I go will point at me, and say, There is the wretch who killed his brother! He was shocked at the thought of this; but not that he had sinned so dreadfully against God! Simon Magus asked Paul to pray that the evils which his sins had deserved, might not come on him, but not that he might be turned from his wicked course. But the true penitent is sorry in his very heart, that he has sinned against God; he not only deplores the sad effects of his sins, but he resolves, in the strength of God's grace, to forsake every thing which does not please God, though it may be as dear to him as a "right hand, or a right eye." [13]

Pharaoh asked Moses to pray, that the frogs might be driven out of the houses, and from the land, the next day. But why would he have them stay till the morrow? Perhaps he thought they might go away of themselves before that time, and that then he should not be obliged to the Lord, or to Moses.

The king said, that when the frogs were removed, then he would let the people go. Bad men, when in sickness, often vow, that they will love and serve God, if he will but remove their trouble; but their hearts are so hard, they do not mind their promises; they get well, forget their vows, and go on in sin as before. This was what Pharaoh did.

Moses said to him, " Be it according to thy word, that thou mayest know, that there is none like the Lord our God." And, truly, there is not; he alone could destroy, or send away the frogs. There is none like him in greatness, for he holds the mighty waters in the hollow of his hand; and he spread abroad the lofty skies. There is none like him in faithfulness; for the heavens and the earth might rather pass away than his word. There

STORY III.

—❋—

THE INSECT ARMY.

BUT though Pharaoh said, that, if God would re-move the plague of the frogs, he would then let the people of Israel go out from the house of their bondage, he would not fulfil his promise. This was adding sin to sin. And when God speaks again and again to any one, and he goes on, and does not mind what God says, his heart gets harder and harder, and more wicked.[1] Thus the bad thoughts, which he delights in, bring forth bad words and actions, which are sin; " and sin, when it is finished, bringeth forth death,"[2] James i. 14, 15. So it was with Pharaoh.

He now became worse and worse. He was so angry with Moses, that he would not see him.

THE INSECT ARMY.

Most likely he bade his servants shut the palace gates, and not permit him to come in any more. And so, perhaps, he vainly thought, that he should not be troubled again about the people of Israel. But God made known to Moses where he might meet with him.

The Lord told him to get up early in the morning. Those who wish to gain knowledge, that they may be useful, and may make the best of life, will rise early, and will not need the command of a master or a parent to do so.[3] They know they must give an account of their time, and they will not waste their precious hours in sloth. God informed his servant Moses, that Pharaoh would go very soon the next morning to the river Nile, to worship it as one of his gods, and that he might meet him there, though he would not suffer him to come into his palace. The Lord not only knows what every one has done, but also what he designs to do. Each may say, He knows my going out, and my coming in, my lying down, and my rising up. " There is not a word on my tongue, or a

thought in my heart, but he knows them altogether.   I cannot go from his Spirit, or flee from his
presence.   The darkness and the light are both
alike to him."   Before him, "the night shineth as
the day."⁴

And Moses went to meet him.   He did not say,
I dare not go; perhaps he will command his guards
to throw me into the river, or to kill me.   No, he
put his trust in the Lord, and he did not care what
the king might do to him.   It is the slothful and
the wicked man, who, when God tells him to do
any thing, says, No, I cannot; " there is a lion in
the way !"⁵

And Moses found Pharaoh where God said he
would, on the brink of the river; and he said,
" Thus saith the Lord, Let my people go, that they
may serve me; else, if thou wilt not let my people
go, behold, I will send swarms of flies upon thee,
and upon thy servants, and upon thy people, and
into thy houses.   But there shall not be any flies
in the land of Goshen, where my people dwell, to
the end thou mayest know, that I am the Lord in

the midst of the earth—and to-morrow shall this sign be."

The flies which God said he would send, were, no doubt, of all kinds; as bees, wasps, gnats, and hornets; for we read in the book of Psalms, that " he sent divers sorts of flies among them which devoured them," Psalm lxxviii. 45.

And the Lord did as he had said he would by his servant Moses. For, at his call, there " came a grievous swarm of flies into the house of Pharaoh, and into the houses of his people, and into all the land of Egypt: and the land was corrupted by reason of them." There is nothing too hard for the Lord to do. And there can be no peace to the wicked. But who are they? They are all those, whether high or low, rich or poor, who will not obey his holy commands.

But none of these dreadful swarms were to be found among the people of Israel. No one could have built a wall to keep out the flies; but God bade them not go into the land of Goshen; and they heard his word, and obeyed it. And he did

so, that the king might know and feel that the
Lord was the great ruler in the midst of the
land.

God is in the midst of every land, and at every
moment; and he was now in Egypt for the defence
of his people.   When once he threatened to send
swarms of hornets among his enemies, he said to
his servants, " But ye shall not be afraid of them;
for the Lord thy God, a mighty God, is among
you," Deut. vii. 20, 21.   And at another time,
when their foes came to make them their prey,
they could not do it.   Then it was said of Israel,
" God is in the midst of her; she shall not be
moved; God shall help her, and that right early,"
Ps. xlvi. 5.   And he did deliver them.

It is not said, as it was when the frogs came up,
that Aaron stretched out his rod; but this rod
could not of itself bring the frogs,—for the Lord
brought them, as well as the flies.   Perhaps the
Lord brought the flies without his servants doing
any thing, that Pharaoh might see, that the judgment did not come by the craft of men, who make

it their business to deceive and cheat people, but by his own Almighty power.

And the wicked king was so stung and plagued by these great swarms of flies and wasps, that he called for Moses, and gave him and the people leave to sacrifice to the Lord, but not out of the land of Egypt. Moses told him, that they could not do so, as God had bade them go into the wilderness; and that, indeed, if this had not been the case, they must needs go out of the land to offer sacrifice, because the people would not endure to see them kill the cattle, which they looked on as among their many gods, but would at once rise and destroy them. Besides, God had said, that he would make known his whole will to the people of Israel, when they were out of Egypt, and not before.

Those who serve God aright come out from the noise and bustle of the world; they separate themselves from the company of the wicked.' " For what communion hath light with darkness? What concord has Christ with Belial? What part hath

my wheat into my garner."[10]   Shall I then be
found among the wheat or the tares?   Solemn
question!

QUESTIONS.

1. When God speaks to any one many times, and he does
not attend, what does his heart become?

2. What does sin do when it is finished?

3. What will those young persons do, who wish to gain
knowledge and to make the best of life?

4. What may each one say, in reference to the knowledge
of God?

5. Who are they who, when God bids them to do any thing,
excuse themselves by saying, there is a lion in the way?

6. Who are the wicked?

7. What do they do who serve God aright?

8. What may all those who love the Lord, say?

9. When the Judge of all shall come, what difference will
he make between the righteous and the wicked?

10. What will the great Husbandman say, in the final
harvest, to the angel reapers?

THE DEPARTURE OF ISRAEL.

STORY IV.

—❋—

THE DEPARTURE OF ISRAEL.

At last, when God had sent his angel to cut off the first-born of all the families of the people of Egypt, Pharaoh let the people go. He was full of alarm, lest he and his subjects should perish. God can compel the mightiest of his foes to " lick the dust before him,"[1] Ps. lxxii. 9.

There was but one way out of Egypt into Canaan, without crossing the Red Sea. This was over a neck of land called Suez. It might have been supposed, that the people would have taken this way, as they had no boats or ships in which they could get over the deep waters. But God " led them by the way of the sea."

We very often see, that God's " thoughts are

not as our thoughts, nor his ways as our ways; but that they are as much above them, as the heavens are above the earth;" and still he says, " I will bring the blind by a way that they know not; I will lead them in paths that they have not known; I will make crooked things straight, and darkness light before them." No one has wisdom enough to choose the way which will be the best for them through life. " It is not in the man that walketh to direct his steps." But we are sure, that every one that humbly asks by fervent prayer, that God would be his guide, shall be " led in the right way, to a city of habitation."*

The nearest way may not always be the right nor the best way. God's way, and God's time, are always the most right, and the best. The farmer would like to reap the harvest almost as soon as he has sown the grain; but he must wait till God shall make it grow and ripen. And the good man would like to see all his prayers answered at once;

---

* Isa. lv. 8, 9; xlii. 16; Jer. x. 23; Ps. cvii. 7.

but it is God's will that he should wait till the proper season.

And God does not lead us in any way without good reason, though we may not know it. He has told us, that he did not lead Israel by the nearest way out of Egypt, because the road lay through a warlike nation ; and they had with them so many women and children, and the people were so un-used to fight, that such a path would have been very trying. " He knoweth our frame, and remem-bereth we are but dust. As a father pitieth his children, so the Lord pitieth them that fear him.' He gathers the lambs in his arms," as the good Shepherd, " and lays them in his bosom." So, he led the people " by a right way."

How glad they must have been to get away from their cruel task-masters ! They had cried for many long years to God to bring them out of Egypt. Had we been there we should have seen every one striving who should be the first to get out of this dreadful country ! Surely, every one, when he was told that he might go, clapped his hands, and

leaped for joy! Surely the whole nation rent the
air with their shouts, and with the high praises of
the Lord! Yet, they marched out of the land in
five large bodies, and in great order. God may
delay to hear the prayer of his people, even when
it is according to his will; but we should never
despair; for, sooner or later, he will be sure to
answer it.[4]

Thus they left the house of their bondage, and
they carried with them all that they had; and, what
was very wonderful, " there was not one feeble
person among their tribes;" that is, among more
than three millions of people.

There was one thing that they took, which we
should have thought they would have left behind;
this was the body of Joseph, who had been dead
about two hundred years. Even the bones of the
dear relatives who have loved us, are precious.
Hence, in not a few places, the graves where they
lie are carefully strewed with fragrant flowers.
The very sight of the coffin of Joseph, would constantly remind them of the vanity of all earthly

grandeur;⁵ for Joseph had been " the Lord of all Egypt;" and now there was nothing remained of him on earth, but these bones, which seemed to say to every one, You too must die, and pass away into eternity!⁶

But it was not on these accounts that the people took with them the bones of Joseph. Nor was it that the earth of the land of Canaan was any better than that of Egypt in which to lay their dead. But it was the last charge of this great and good man that they should do so. " I die;" said he to his brethren, " and God will surely visit you, and bring you out of this land unto the land which he sware to Abraham, to Isaac, and to Jacob."⁷ And he took an oath of the children of Israel, saying, " God will surely visit you, and ye shall carry up my bones from hence," Gen. 1. 24, 25. Hence the Apostle says, " By faith, Joseph, when he was dying, made mention of the departing of the children of Israel; and gave commandment concerning his bones," Heb. xi. 22. The very sight of these bones would remind the tribes of Israel of

D

the great promise of God to give them the land of Canaan, " the goodly land, flowing with milk and honey."

But how could they find their way through the vast desert which lay between them and the goodly land? Why, " the Lord went before them, by day in a pillar of cloud, to lead them in the way ; and by night in a pillar of fire, to give them light; to go by day and night: he took not away the pillar of the cloud by day, nor the pillar of fire by night, from before the people,"⁸ Exod. xiii. 21, 22.

God bade them, by his servant Moses, follow the leading of the pillar of cloud; when this rose, they were to rise and follow it; and when it stood still, they were to pitch their camp and repose.⁹ If any should have said, We will not go on in the way in which the pillar of cloud directs; or, we will not rest when it stands still, but we will go which way we please, and rest when and where we please, they would have been lost; they would have perished in that vast wilderness. There is but one way out of this world of sin and sorrow,—

it is the way of holiness,[10]—God has bid every one walk in it; and he who does not ask for the aids of God's Spirit, that he may do so, will perish in his sins![11] Lord, let it not be the case with me!

The pillar of cloud, and of fire, must have given the people great comfort and joy, for they made it evident, that God was very near to them, and at every moment.[12] They had only to lift up their eyes to see that this was the case. Hence Moses said to them, " What nation is there so great, who hath God so nigh to them, as the Lord our God is, in all things that we call upon him for?" God is now the same to every one of his praying people. He says to each of them, " My presence shall go with thee, and I will give thee rest! I will never leave thee, nor forsake thee!"[13]

Each day, the pillar of cloud led their way, and shaded them from the fierce beams of the sun; and each night the pillar of fire lit them on their march, or in their tents, and cheered them by its warmth. It would have been very sad for them, if they had been guided only for a season, and then left to find their way themselves. God's mercies follow us, like a never-failing stream, through the wilderness;[14] they are not only " new every morning, but they are renewed every evening," and every moment. Well does Philip Henry say, " We were undone, if the end of one mercy were not the beginning of another."[15]

And did the pillar of cloud shelter the people from the fierce rays of the sun? How does this remind us of our Saviour,[16] who is, to all who believe in him, as " the shadow of a great rock in a weary land." If he had not stood between us, and received on himself the dreadful wrath of God, so justly due to our sins, it would have fallen upon us, and would have consumed us utterly![17]

QUESTIONS.

1. What can God compel the mightiest of his foes to do?
2. Of what are we quite sure?
3. How does the Lord pity his servants?
4. What should we never do, though God may delay to answer the prayers of his people?

5. Of what would the coffin of Joseph constantly remind Israel?

6. What did his bones seem to say?

7. What did Joseph say, when dying, to his brethren?

8. How did the Lord guide his people through the vast desert of Arabia?

9. What were the people to do, when the cloud arose, and when it rested?

10. Which is the right way to a better world?

11. What will be the end of the man who does not walk in it?

12. What did the pillars of cloud and fire make evident?

13. What does God say to every praying soul?

14. How do God's mercies follow us?

15. What does Philip Henry say of them?

16. Of whom does the shade which the pillar of cloud afforded, remind us?

17. If Christ had not borne the wrath of God due to our sins, what would have become us?

STORY V.

—✳—

THE GIVING OF THE LAW.

PART I.

AFTER Pharaoh had let the people of Israel go out of his land, God opened a passage for them through the Red Sea, and they took their journey by the wilderness. And, as they had no corn-fields, gardens, or vineyards, and could not provide themselves with food, they must all have been starved but for God's great goodness. He gave them showers of bread from heaven, which they called Manna; and they gathered it up every morning and evening. He also spake to the fowls, and bade them come up to the camp of the people in great plenty; and they came at his call. So God spread for them a table, and covered it with choice

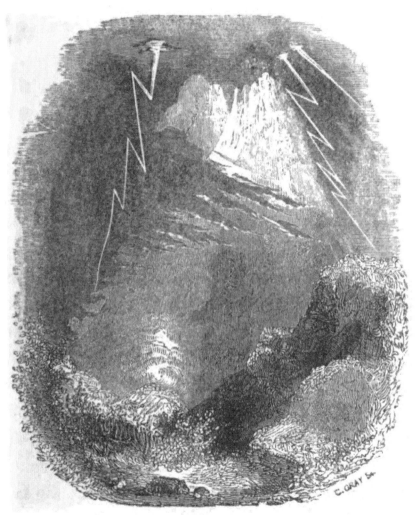

THE GIVING OF THE LAW.

food, where no hand but his could have done it, in the barren wilderness.[1] He is as able now as he was then, and as willing too, to supply the wants of those who put their trust in him.

When the people had been on their journey a little more than two months, they came to a large mountain, that had two peaks; the name of one was Horeb, and that of the other Sinai: and they set up their camp before this mountain. The thick cloud from which God had spoken, rested on the top of it; and God called Moses up to converse with him. This was a great honour, and it is one which God gives to all his servants; for all may speak to him, when they please, by prayer.[2]

And God told Moses to remind the people, as they were very apt to forget, of the great things which he had done on their behalf; how he had brought them out of their " house of bondage;" how he had punished their foes; how, by his pillar of cloud rolling before, and his pillar of fire bringing up their rear, he had put a wall between them and their enemies, which they could not break through; and how tenderly he had watched over them; and had borne them so much on high, out of the reach of the arrows that were hurled at them, as on the wings of an eagle.

And ought not we often to think, how goodly a land the Lord our God has given to us? Ought we not to be thankful to him for bread to eat, and raiment to put on; for his kind care over us by night and by day; for his precious word; and, above all, for Christ Jesus, his unspeakable gift? Truly we ought.

And God told Moses, that, since he had done so much good for the people, he expected that they, in return, would obey his voice, and serve him; and it was very right they should do so. The owner of the vineyard came year after year, expecting to meet with fruit on every tree; but there was one on which he did not find any; and he was very angry, and bade his servants cut it down; "Why," said he, "cumbereth it the ground?"

When a parent teaches a child what he should know, and takes all the pains and care he can with

him, he expects, that he should obey his commands, and try to please him by his temper and
conduct.' And should not this be the case with
the children of God? It should. O that God
would give me the teachings of his Holy Spirit,
that I might love and serve him!

Though God charged the people to obey his
voice, and he had a right to do so, yet he did not
need their praises or their services, "for the earth
is his, and the fulness thereof, the world and they
who dwell therein;" and there could be no reason
why he should concern himself about a poor nation
whom he had brought out of slavery, but his own
goodness.

Israel was bound to serve God, because he had
loved them as a man loves that which he deems his
choicest treasure.' And so, in every age, he loves
all who love him; and each one should serve him,
even as those who are set apart for his worship.
All his true servants are "a chosen generation, a
royal priesthood, a peculiar people;" and they
should "show forth his praise who has called them

out of darkness into his marvellous light,"' 1 Pet.
ii. 9.   And, let each ask himself, Do I thus serve
him ?

So Moses told the people all that the Lord had
said; and they all answered, " All that the Lord
hath spoken, will we do."   We should not only
say,—we should pray for grace that we may really
do it.   For, they who know their Lord's will, and
do it not, we are assured, will not only be punished,
but will " be beaten with many stripes." ⁸

And now God was about really to give his law
to Israel, he told Moses, that he would come down
from heaven in the sight of the people.   But did
he do so?   And could they indeed see God ?   No;
" No man hath seen God at any time ;" and no man
can see him and live.   What, then, did the Lord
mean ?   That he would display before them so
much of his glory, as should fill them with a solemn
awe, and convince them, that he alone had a right
to claim their worship and love.

This was a great sight; and the people were to
spend three days in preparing for it.   And how

did they spend this time ? Most likely, in thinking and speaking of God : of his power, wisdom,
goodness, and mercy ; of what he had done for
them, and of what he had promised to do. In
prayer and praise, and holy desire that they might
serve him all the days of their lives.' Lord, bestow
on me thy grace, that I may thus think, and thus
serve thee !

At this solemn period Moses told the people,
that they were not to go too near the mountain.
" Take heed," said he, " to yourselves, that ye go
not up into the mount, or touch the border of it :
there shall not a hand touch it, but he shall surely
be stoned, or shot through ; whether it be beast
or man, it shall not live ; only when the trumpet
soundeth long, they shall then come up to the
mount."

At length the millions of the people were brought
near by Moses. " It came to pass on the third day
in the morning, that there were thunders and light-
nings, and a thick cloud upon the mount, and the
voice of the trumpet exceeding loud ; so that all

the people who were in the camp trembled. And Moses brought forth the people out of the camp to meet with God. And mount Sinai was altogether on a smoke, because the Lord descended on it in fire: and the smoke thereof ascended as the smoke of the furnace; and the whole mount quaked greatly. And when the voice of the trumpet sounded long, and waxed louder and louder, Moses spake, and God answered him by a voice. And the Lord came down upon mount Sinai, on the top of the mount; and Moses went up." How should we pray for grace that we may serve God with reverence and godly fear! [10]

And now, at this solemn moment, God gave his holy law unto the people. " He spake to them all these words; I am the Lord thy God, which have brought thee out of the land of Egypt, out of the house of bondage." When a master or a parent speaks, how carefully we ought to hear; and how much more so when God himself deigns to speak to us; and how ought we to lay up his words in our memory. A great king once said to God, " The law of thy mouth is better unto me than thousands of gold and silver;"[11] and if we think as we ought, we shall say so too.

God told the people, that he was Jehovah, the only living and true God, the creator of all things; and that, therefore, he had a right to command them what they should do, and what they should avoid. He also said, that he was "their God." All will be well, and for ever well, with those who have God for their God. And if we look up to him by prayer, and ask him for Christ's sake, to be our God, he will be sure to hear us. And then we shall be more rich than a man who could say of a great mountain of gold, It is mine![12] For he would be our friend, who made all the gold and silver in the world, and even the world itself!

God said, that he had brought them " out of the land of Egypt," a land full of idols, and wickedness; and out " of the house of bondage." He had suffered them to be tried, to humble them, to bring them to call upon him, to make them willing to leave Egypt; and to display his power and glory to the nations as their God. Troubles do not " come by chance, or spring out of the ground."

God brought them out of this land. Their enemies were so many and so mighty, that no hand but his could bring them out. It was when they were ready to perish, that he came down to deliver them. And he changed the shadow of death with which they were covered, into the bright beams of the morning. Nothing is too hard for him to do." No one who trusts in God, should say, " I shall one day fall by the hand of my enemy;" because, with such a helper, no one can fall. And he has said to his servants, " Call on me in the day of trouble, I will deliver thee, and thou shalt glorify me," Ps. l. 15.

To live in sin is to live in the house of bondage. Sin rules as a dreadful task-master over the body and soul. And his servants we are whom we obey. The slaves of sin are the worst of slaves; for all who serve sin and Satan now, will be wretched both in this world, and in that which is to come, and that too for ever. But the servants of the

Lord are all brought by his grace and spirit out of " the house of bondage." " Being made free from sin, they have their fruit unto holiness, and the end everlasting life,"[13] Rom. vi. 22.

~~~~~~~~~~~~~~~~~~~

QUESTIONS.

1. What did God do for the people of Israel in the barren wilderness?

2. What is the honour which God confers on all his servants?

3. For what ought we to be thankful?

4. What does a parent expect in return for his care of his child?

5. How did God love his Israel?

6. What are the Lord's true servants?

7. And what should they do?

8. What will be the portion of those who know the Lord's will, and do it not?

9. In what manner did the people prepare to meet God?

10. How should we serve God?

11. What did a great king once say to God?

12. Than whom shall we be richer if God be our God?

13. From what are God's servants made free?

lips only, he will not hear them,—nor can they be pleasing in his sight.

The third commandment which God gave, was, " Thou shalt not take the name of the Lord thy God in vain, for the Lord will not hold him guiltless, that taketh his name in vain."[5]

And what must I do to keep this commandment? I must not mention the name of God, even in my prayers, without thinking how great and glorious, and holy he is ; I must not make a jest of his holy word, or of any thing sacred; I must not lightly say, O God, or O Christ, or curse or swear as wicked people do:[6] or else God will be sure to punish me : but I must be often using my tongue to speak of his glory, and to show forth his loving-kindness and his tender-mercy.[7] And do I indeed do so ?

The fourth commandment which God gave was, " Remember the sabbath-day to keep it holy."[8] And what must I do to keep this commandment? I must spend the whole day in the service of God; in prayer and in praise ; in waiting on him in his public courts, in hearing his word, and in doing his holy will.[9]

Then they do not keep God's holy day as they ought, who do their usual work, who buy and sell, or settle their accounts, who stay at home needlessly, or who go out on parties of pleasure. The horse or the cow keeps the sabbath as well as those who cease from their labour, but who do not serve God.[10]

They who go to sleep in the house of God, or who do not mind what the minister says, do not keep the sabbath-day holy.[11] And they who do not hallow the sabbath, do not love God, and are not of the number of his children.

The fifth commandment which God gave was, " Honour thy father and thy mother, that thy days may be long in the land which the Lord thy God giveth thee."[12]

He who obeys this command, loves his parents, and does as they bid him, unless their wishes are contrary to the will of God. Should they be poor and ill, he will try and help them, and do them all manner of good. He will imitate the example of the Lord Jesus ;—

> " Who, tho' he reigns above the sky,
>   And keeps the world in awe,
> Was once a child as young as I,
>   And kept his Father's law.

> " At twelve years old he talk'd with men,
>   (The Jews all wond'ring stand,)
> Yet he obey'd his mother then,
>   And came at her command." [13]

He will also obey the lawful commands of his teachers and superiors. To such God has given his blessing in many ways,—whilst he has frowned on undutiful and wicked children, and many of them have been cut off in their sins. [14]

The sixth commandment which God gave was, " Thou shalt do no murder." [15] He who keeps this command, not only does not kill any one, but is meek, and kind to all; he is not angry with his brother, nor does he hate any one. In this, as well as in every other duty, the Lord Jesus has set us an example; for " when he was reviled, he re-

viled not again; when he was rebuked, he threatened not; but committed himself to him who judged
righteously."[16]

"Thou shalt not commit adultery,"[17] was the
seventh commandment which God gave; and
which forbids all improper and filthy thoughts,
words, and actions.

"Thou shalt not steal,"[18] was the eighth commandment which God gave. This, and all God's
commands, are very right; for we should not like
for any one to take any thing away from us; and,
therefore, we should not take any thing from
others.[19]

To keep this command as we ought, we should
not only be honest towards our fellow-creatures,
but we must give to God that which is his due.

The hours of the Lord's day are his; and he robs
God who does not devote them to his praise."[20]

Our powers of body and mind are his, for he
created them, and he preserves them every moment; and he robs God, who does not give him
the love of his heart, and the obedience of his life."[21]

All the good which we possess was given us by God; and he robs him, who can see his fellow-creatures in want or trouble, and does not do any thing for their relief.

He who does not praise God from his heart, for all the mercies which he bestows on him, robs God of that which is his just due." Each one should every day pray for grace, that he may not break the command, " Thou shalt not steal !"

" Thou shalt not bear false witness against thy neighbour," is the ninth commandment which God gave. It is worthy of notice, that two out of the ten commands have reference to the government of the tongue." No doubt this was, because God knew, that people were very apt to offend with their tongues, and this is, indeed, the case. And as none are pleased that any should bear false witness against them, so they ought to take heed, and say nothing of their fellow-creatures but what is strictly true. This command plainly condemns the liar. Whatever trouble or pain any one may come into by telling the truth, he will be sure to

fall into much greater by telling falsehoods. Whatever may happen, every one should speak the
truth :

"For liars we can never trust,
    Tho' they should speak the thing that's true;
And he that does one fault at first,
    And lies to hide it, makes it two.[34]

" Then let me always watch my lips,
    Lest I be struck to death and hell;
Since God a book of reck'ning keeps,
    For every lie that children tell."[35]

" Thou shalt not covet any thing that is thy
neighbour's,"[36] is the tenth, and last commandment
which God gave. Then it appears, from this pre-
cept, that any one may break God's commands,
and be a sinner before him, though he may not do
so openly. If we do not obey his will even in our
thoughts, we are guilty. Then how true is that
scripture which says, " There is none righteous,—
no, not one." And how earnestly should we pray,
" Lord, have mercy upon us,—and write all these
thy laws in our hearts, we humbly beseech thee!"[37]

All then have broken this holy and righteous law of God, and are liable to be punished for their sins. " For if we say we have no sin, we only deceive ourselves, and the truth is not in us." So, all are justly exposed to the anger of God."** For it is written, " Cursed is every one that continueth not in all things, which are written in the book of the law to do them." No one can make amends for his past misdeeds, because he can never do more than his duty."* And if God were not to punish any one for breaking his law, he would not be a just or holy being, and his laws would be only advice,—and not of so much importance as the laws which are made by men. Nor can any one suffer the penalty due to the breaker of the law without being miserable for ever.

How then can any one be saved? Not by any thing he can do, or suffer, or by his own works of any kind. For if, as the Apostle says, " righteousness," or a good title to heaven, come, " by the works of the law," or by any obedience which the sinner can perform, then " is Christ dead in vain;"

there was no occasion for Christ to have died, if men could have saved themselves.

How, then, can any one be saved? By faith in the merits of the Lord Jesus." "God so loved the world, that he gave his only-begotten Son, that whosoever believeth in him might not perish, but have everlasting life." [31] In him God is "a just God, and yet a Saviour;" in him, "mercy and truth have met together, righteousness and peace have kissed each other." "Christ hath redeemed us from the curse of the law, having become a curse for us," by dying on the cross.[32] And "it is," says the Apostle, "a faithful saying, and worthy of all acceptation, that Jesus Christ came into the world to save sinners, of whom I am chief." By faith in him, therefore, we are justified from all things, from which we could not be justified by the law of Moses." [33] Well may we therefore say,

> " My soul, no more attempt to draw,
> Thy life, or comfort from the law;
> Fly to the hope the Gospel gives,
> The soul that trusts the promise lives !" [34]

QUESTIONS.

1. What is the first commandment?
2. What must you give to God?
3. What is the second commandment?
4. How must you think of God?
5. What is the third commandment?
6. What must you not lightly say?
7. How must you be often using your tongue?
8. What is the fourth commandment?
9. How must you keep the Lord's day?
10. What creatures keep the sabbath as well as those who do not serve God?
11. Do they who sleep in the house of God, and who do not mind what the minister says, keep the sabbath-day holy?
12. What is the fifth commandment?
13. What did Jesus do when he was twelve years of age?
14. How has God dealt with undutiful and wicked children?
15. What is the sixth commandment?
16. How did the Lord Jesus act when he was reviled?
17. What is the seventh commandment?
18. What is the eighth commandment?
19. What should we not like any one to do to us?
20. Who is he who robs God?
21. What is the ninth commandment?
22. Which two commandments have reference to the government of the tongue?

23. What should we all do whatever may happen?

24. Whom can we never trust?

25. What should we always do?

26. What is the tenth commandment

27. How should we earnestly pray?

28. To what are all justly exposed on account of their sins?

29. Why can we never make amends for our past sins?

30. How can any one be saved?

31. How has God loved the world?

32. How has Christ redeemed us from the curse of the law?

33. How are we justified from every charge?

34. What may we well say?

STORY VII.

—✻—

MORE ABOUT JOB.

PART I.

You have read in the second series of the Bible Story Book about Job, and how great his troubles were; and his patience was as great as his troubles. And now you shall hear about the end of his life.

His friends were angry with him, and tried to convince him that he was a bad man, or else he would not have been so much afflicted. They asked him a great number of questions, and Job answered them. Thus they went on for a long time; but after all their talking they could not agree; and they might have gone on in this way till the present time, had they lived, if God had not settled the dispute. But he did so; he spake

JOB, IN HIS PROSPERITY.

to Job out of the whirlwind. Job had said in his
defence, too much about his own knowledge and
goodness. And now God asked him many questions, and so made him feel what a poor ignorant
creature he was before his Maker. This is plain
from what he at last said to God,—indeed he was
so much surprised, that he could not for a long
while say any thing.

But, at last, he looked up to God, and he said,
" O Lord, I know that thou canst do every thing,
and no thought can be withholden from thee."[1]
Many, even of the Lord's servants, have been ready
to think, that he could not, or would not, provide
for, or help them. His Israel, who had seen the
wonders of his power so often, said, " Can God
spread for us a table in the wilderness?" And
Moses, at one time, seemed to think the same.
But there is nothing which is too hard for the
Lord to do. His arms of almighty love can support us under the heaviest trials, and bring us out
of them. He can spread, for he has done it, a
table for us in the very sight of our foes. The

cattle upon a thousand hills are all his own. All creatures are his servants; he bade the ravens feed Elijah when he was in the wilderness. "He can do exceedingly beyond all we can ask, or even think." He can pardon and save the poor sinner who comes to him through Christ, and can change him into an angel of light.' And, what is more, we are sure that he will do it.

God can do every thing; and he knows every thing. "I know," says he, "the thoughts that come into your heart, every one of them." David said, "Lord, thou hast searched me, and known me; thou knowest my down-sitting, and up-rising; there is not a word on my tongue, or a thought in my heart, but lo, O Lord, thou art acquainted with them altogether."' He knows, all our good thoughts, and he approves of them; and he knows all our bad thoughts, and he hates them. How should we be humbled before him. How should we watch over our hearts with holy diligence! How earnestly should we breathe the prayer contained in the following lines:—

" O may these thoughts possess my breast,
   Where'er I rove, where'er I rest;
   Nor let my weaker passions dare
   Consent to sin, for God is there!" [4]

Job confessed his ignorance before God; how he had been so foolish, and so sinful, as to utter things about God's dealings which he " had not understood." He had talked with his friends just as if the Lord destroyed the innocent; when we know that he would not do it: just as if he had not deserved his afflictions: without thinking, that it was of the Lord's mercies that he was not consumed; without thinking, that God had a right to do with him as he pleased. He had spoken, and he was sorry for it, just as if he had a right to direct God how he should govern his creatures. But now he was convinced of his ignorance and pride in so doing. How should we say, as one did in old time, " I will take heed to my ways, that I offend not with my tongue." [5]

And now God had shown him more of his power and grandeur, and more of his holiness and justice, he felt as he had never done before; and he said, " I have heard of thee by the hearing of the ear, but now mine eye seeth thee, 1 repent, and abhor myself in dust and ashes." [6] Those then who have high and proud thoughts of themselves, do not know God aright; for they who know him " abhor" themselves. " I abhor myself!" said Job. What a weighty word is this? I abhor myself, for having found fault of God's conduct towards his creatures; I abhor myself, for boasting before him of my own righteousness and goodness; I abhor myself, for saying and thinking, that in afflicting me, he has designed any thing but my good; and I abhor myself for all my sins of thought, word, and deed, which are so many, that they cannot be numbered. " I repent,"—my mind is entirely changed about God and his ways, and my own character; I would seek his mercy above all things; and I wish humbly to love and serve him all the days of my life. And do I wish to do so too?

And do I know any thing of that sorrow of heart

for my sins which Job felt? God's servants have
always abhorred themselves before him.' Abraham
did so. "Be not angry," said he, "that I, who
am but dust and ashes, have taken upon me to
speak unto the Lord." Mary did so, when she
washed the Saviour's feet with her tears, and wiped
them with the hairs of her head. The poor woman
did so, who was content to be ranked with the dogs
which gathered the crumbs under the children's
table. He did so, who would not so much as lift
up his eyes unto heaven, but smote upon his breast,
and said, "God be merciful to me, a sinner!"
And so did the broken-hearted Prodigal who said
to his Father, who ran to meet and to welcome
him, "I have sinned against heaven, and in thy
sight, and am no more worthy to be called thy
son; make me as one of thy hired servants!"

And, reader, are these the feelings of thy heart?
Dost thou so know God as to abhor thyself before
him on account of thy sins? Then God has sent
a message to thee,—and it is,—" The heaven is
my throne, and the earth is my footstool; but

F

to this man will I look, even to him that is poor, and of a contrite spirit, and that trembleth at my word."⁹

~~~~~~~~~

QUESTIONS.

1. What did Job say at last?

2. What can God do?

3. What did David say?

4. What is the prayer we should offer in reference to God's knowledge of us?

5. What should we say about our tongues?

6. What did Job say, of God, and of himself?

7. What have God's servants always done before him?

8. What did Abraham, and the Publican, and the Prodigal, say?

9. And what does God say to the true penitent?

STORY VIII.

—✿—

MORE ABOUT JOB.

PART II.

WHEN Job humbled himself before God, and confessed his sins, the Lord spoke peace and pardon to him. No one, besides the Lord, can heal the wounded spirit.

And the Lord was pleased with him, and seemed to delight in calling him his servant, which he does four times in two verses. Satan accused Job before God as a hypocrite, and he said he would prove it; but after all he could do, he failed. The great enemy was " a liar from the beginning ;" and he is still the same. God will sooner or later vindicate the characters of his servants. Let them humbly and calmly commit their way to

F 2

him. " Vengeance is mine, I will repay, saith the Lord !"

It is a great honour to serve an earthly monarch; what then, must it be, to be a servant of the King of kings? And am I his servant? Am I trying, in the strength of his grace, to think and to act in such a way, as shall be pleasing in his sight?[1] His servants serve him with delight, as children who love their father, and not as a slave;[2] they wish to obey not only some, but all his command- ments; they serve him with holy diligence, and they desire thus to serve him for ever.[3] And do I thus serve him? If I do, all will be well with me, both here and hereafter; for the Lord will provide for his servants all needful good; he will give them strength and grace equal to their day; and he will afterwards bring them to glory.[4]

But the Lord was displeased with the friends of Job; for they had not spoken of him as they ought to have done; and they judged Job very harshly, since they thought he was a hypocrite, and said so, and tried all they could to prove it. If God approve oi us, we need not be much concerned about what our fellow-creatures may say.' God is justly displeased with those who do not think and speak of others with much kindness and mercy.' This is not doing to others as they would be done unto.

So the Lord said to Eliphaz, " My wrath is kindled against thee, and against thy two friends; for ye have not spoken of me the thing that is right, as my servant Job hath. Therefore, take unto you now seven bullocks and seven rams, and go to my servant Job, and offer up for yourselves a burnt-offering; and my servant Job shall pray for you; for him will I accept, lest I deal with you after your folly," or sin.

They were to go to Job; this would humble and mortify them; for they had proudly thought themselves much better than he was, whom they treated as a hypocrite. " He that exalteth himself shall be abased, but he that humbleth himself shall be exalted."

- They were to offer " seven bullocks, and seven rams." These were to be slain, and wholly burnt;

to show, that the sinner deserved to be consumed
by God's justice ;' but that, as God accepted the
offering, and let the sinner go free,—so, for the
merits' sake of his dear Son, who died on the cross
for guilty rebels, he would accept, pardon, and
save the most unworthy. So Noah and Abraham
offered up animals as a sacrifice; not that the blood
of bulls and goats could take away sin; for the
Apostle says, it could not do so; yet without the
shedding of blood there could be no remission.
But the blood of these animals was an emblem of
that precious blood which was shed upon the cross,
and which does cleanse from all sin.* '

Job was to pray for his friends that God would
accept their offering, and that he would pardon and
bless them. And God said, that he would accept
them in answer to his plea. So God does forgive and bless and save any poor sinner who asks
him to do so for Christ's sake. And so the
Saviour, who is our great High Priest, pleads

* Heb. x. 1—10; 1 John i. 7.

for all who commit their cause into his gracious hands.'

The friends of Job " went and did as the Lord commanded." Whatever the Lord bids us do, we should do it. And if the command be hard, we should ask him to give us his strength and grace, and these will make the most difficult duty easy.¹⁰ When God bade Abraham offer up his son, he arose, and went on his way to the Mount of Moriah to do it; and God was pleased with his ready obedience, though he did not permit him to sacrifice his son. " Now," said he, " I know that thou fearest me, since thou hast not withheld thy son, thy only son, from me."

The Lord requires the most exact obedience. God gave his command, that the ark was to be brought up to Jerusalem on men's shoulders; instead of this, the people placed it on a new cart, and God was displeased with them. We must not only do what God commands, but we must do it in the way in which he directs.

And the Lord accepted Job, according to his

promise. He cannot be worse than his word. The heavens and the earth might rather pass away, than this be the case. It is the glory of the Divine Being, as the Apostle says, that " he cannot lie!"[11] so that

> " If he speaks a promise once,
> The eternal grace is sure."

When our persons are accepted by God for Christ's sake, then our prayers and our offerings will be accepted also.[12] But not otherwise. Thus we read, that " Cain brought of the fruit of the ground, an offering unto the Lord. And Abel, he also brought of the firstlings of his flock, and of the fat thereof. And the Lord had respect unto Abel, and to his offering ; but unto Cain and his offering he had not respect."

If the Lord accepted the friends of Job for his sake, how much the more will he accept the poor sinner who comes to him for Christ's sake. " This," said he, " is my beloved Son, in whom I am well pleased." And he is " the Head of his body, the church ;" and if he be well-pleased with the Head, will he not be so with the whole body? We are sure that he will.[13]

QUESTIONS.

1. What am I trying to do if I am a servant of the Lord?
2. How do his servants serve him?
3. How do they wish to obey his commands, and to serve him?
4. What will the Lord do for his servants?
5. If God approve of us, what need we not mind?
6. With whom is God justly displeased?
7. Why were sacrifices to be burnt?
8. Of what was the blood of animals an emblem?
9. For whom does the Saviour plead?
10. What will the grace and strength of Christ do?
11. What is the glory of the Divine Being?
12. How may we know if God accepts our offerings?
13. As God is well pleased with his Son, who is the head of the church, will he not be so with the whole body?

STORY IX.

—✳—

MORE ABOUT JOB.

PART III.

At length the Lord brought Job out of his great troubles, when he had made trial of his faith and patience. We must not forget, that it is the Lord who supports us in affliction, and who brings us out of it. The waves of trouble would drown us, if the Lord did not say to them, " Hitherto shall ye come, but no further!" And how readily can he stop or turn them back. There is no disease which he cannot cure. He healed the poor man at the pool of Bethesda, and with a word, who had been ill thirty and eight years.[1]

It was when Job prayed for his friends, that the Lord brought him out of his trials. We are doing what is pleasing in his sight, when we pray for others, and try to do them good.' Do I pray for my dear parents, and for my brothers and sisters?

And the Lord heard his prayer for his friends, and forgave their sins, in answer to it. He does hear the fervent prayer of a righteous man, offered to him for the merits' sake of his dear Son.'

And was it not very kind of Job to pray for his friends, who had treated him so very ill? It was. He had a portion of his temper, who, on the cross, prayed for his murderers, and said, "Father, forgive them; they know not what they do!" And we should forgive those who have done us the most harm, even as God, for Christ's sake, forgives us."'

The Lord not only heard Job's prayer, but he gave him, what he could never have asked him for, even "twice" as much as he had before his troubles. They that honour God, he will be sure sooner or later to honour. And see how able he is to do "exceeding abundantly beyond all we can ask or think."'

And now when he had again become great and rich, his " sisters and brethren," who had not visited him in trouble, came to see and to comfort him. Earthly friends sometimes are unkind, and forsake us when we most need them. But there is a friend, " who sticketh closer than a brother ;" who always loves those who love him, and at all times ; this friend, who never changes, is God.⁶

It is very wrong to desert our friends in trouble or in want; or to give them only a mouthful of good words, when they need food, and raiment, and medicine. " He who hath this world's good, and seeth his brother hath need, and shutteth up the bowels of his compassion from him, how," says the Apostle John, " dwelleth the love of God in him ?"⁷

And the Lord blessed Job, and made him very happy in his latter days. We may wish and pray, and strive, that our friends may be blessed, but God alone can bless them. He can bring, and with a word, from weakness to strength, from sickness to health, from poverty to riches, and from a

place on a dunghill to a throne. He can change
darkness into light, disgrace into honour, and death
into life.

But a man may be rich, and yet not blessed.
He may have health and honour, friends and pleasures, and all kinds of worldly good, and yet not
be blessed.' There are many such people in the
world. But there are also very many whom the
Lord blesses; and they are happy, though they
may be sick, and poor, and despised, or on a dying
bed. And who are they? They are those who
love God, and trust in the merits of the Lord
Jesus for salvation; who pray for all the blessings
they need, and who are always trying to please
him, in all they say, and do.' And am I one of
these blessed people?

So the Lord blessed Job more at the latter end
of his life, than at the beginning. And it is often
the case with God's servants, that their last days
are their best, and their happiest. It was so with
Jacob, with Joseph, and with David, as well as
Job. " The path of the just is as the shining

light, which shineth more and more unto the perfect day." " Mark the perfect man, and behold the upright, for the end of that man is peace." [10]

At last, Job reached the close of his life; and he died full of days, and full of wealth, and honours. Death concludes the history of every one. All must lie down and die. " By one man sin entered into the world, and death by sin, and so death passed upon all, for that all have sinned." [11]

So he was gathered into the heavenly garner, " as a shock of corn is gathered in its season, fully ripe."

Happy is the man, who, like Job, " is old, and full of days;" and is ready to leave this world for a better. When the voice is heard that calls him into eternity, he will say, as Simeon did, " Lord, now lettest thou thy servant depart in peace, for mine eyes have seen thy salvation!" [12]

QUESTIONS.

1. How did our Lord heal the poor man, who had been ill thirty-eight years?

2. When we pray for others, and try to do them good, what are we doing?

3. What does God hear?

4. How should we forgive those who have done us harm?

5. What is God able to do?

6. Mention the friend who always loves those who love him, and at all times?

7. What does St. John say of relieving the needy?

8. What may a man be and have, and not be blessed?

9. Who are they whom the Lord blesses?

10. Whom should we mark?

11. How did sin and death come into the world?

12. What did Simeon say?

STORY X.

—✳—

THE KING AND THE FALSE PROPHET.

PART I.

BALAK, the king of Moab, heard that the people of Israel were coming near his country, and he and his subjects were very much afraid; for they had been told how, by the help of their God, they had cut off many wicked nations.

The king did not know what to do; but after thinking some time, he resolved by some craft to get their God not to care for them any longer; and then he thought he could do what he pleased with them.

He had heard of a famous man, who pretended to be religious, whose name was Balaam; he lived at a great distance from Moab. This false teacher,

THE KING AND THE FALSE PROPHET.

it had been said, could curse or bless people as he
chose; so, as he feared the people of Israel would
" devour all that was in his kingdom, even," to use
his own words, " as the ox licketh up the grass of
the field," he sent to him ; and this was his message, " Come, I pray thee, curse me this people,
for they are too mighty for me, that we may smite
them, and drive them out of the land; for I wot
that he whom thou blessest is blessed, and he
whom thou cursest is cursed."

But it was not as the king thought.　The curses
of a wicked man can never hurt those who trust in
God.[1]　When the great giant Goliath saw David,
who was but a youth, " coming against him, with
five smooth stones from the brook," and a sling,
" he disdained him, and cursed him by his gods."
And he said, he would tear him in pieces, and
" give his flesh to the beasts of the field, and the
fowls of the air."　But David threw a stone, which
beat in his forehead, and killed him ; and he ran,
and got on him, and pulled out the giant's sword,
and cut off his head.　And so it always will be :

G

the curse of a wicked man shall never hurt a servant of the living God.

To make this false prophet come and curse Israel, Balak sent him a present of money. " The love of money is the root of all evil." Judas sold Christ for thirty pieces of silver, and was, at last, cast into hell for his covetousness.[2] What then did he gain by it?

Balaam wanted to have this money; and he was very willing to curse God's people, that he might get it. So he bade the persons who were sent to him, to stay till the morning. He ought to have sent them away at once, telling them, that he would never be so wicked as to curse the servants of the Most High. If we do not resist sin at once, we are in great danger of falling into it, and of being ruined.[3] We should never pause for an instant to ask the question, Shall I disobey the commandment of God? But we should say, with Joseph, " How can I do this great wickedness, and sin against him?"

In the night, God spoke to Balaam; of course,

he did not see him; "for no man hath seen God at any time;" but in the silence of the night he heard the voice of the Most High in his chamber, and it said, "Thou shalt not go to Balak; thou shalt not curse the people, for they are blessed."

So, when he rose in the morning, he told the servants of the king, that the Lord would not give him leave to go with them. But he did not tell them, that Israel was a people blessed by God, and that he would not let any one curse them. Wicked ministers never say all to the people which God has bid them.

Balak was so resolved that Balaam should curse the people, that he would not take the refusal: and he sent to him again by princes of a higher rank; and, no doubt, they took with them more money, and promised him greater honours: and his second message was more earnest than the first. "Let nothing," said he, " I pray thee, hinder thee from coming to me. For I will promote thee unto very great honour; and I will do whatsoever thou sayest unto me; come, therefore, I pray thee, curse

me this people !"   Whatever gain may be offered
us, if we feel as we ought, we shall refuse to go in
any way which is forbidden by the holy word of
God.⁴

And, at first, Balaam spoke very well.   " If
Balak," said he, " would give me his house full of
silver and gold, I cannot go beyond the word of the
Lord my God."   If we had heard him speak thus,
we should have thought, that gold and silver were
as nothing to him, and that the will of God was
every thing: but it was not so.   Men must be
judged now, as they will at the great day, by their
actions, and not by their words.⁵

This wicked prince wanted to go to Balak ; and
so he kept the messengers, as he did before, all
night ; to see if God would speak to him again,
and let him go.   As if God would change his mind,
and curse those to-day whom he had yesterday
blessed !   Perhaps he asked God to give him leave
to go ; which was the same as begging leave to
despise his commands, and to sin against him,
And how shocking was all this !

And the Lord was not pleased with him; but to confound the idol gods of Moab, and to answer his own wise purposes, he suffered him to go. No wicked man can say, or do any thing, without the Lord's permission.ᵉ And God told Balaam that it was at his peril, to say any thing which he should not bid him.

He was now so eager to go to Balak, that he rose up early, before the princes were stirring, and got ready for his journey. He also took two of his servants with him. It seems likely that the messengers set off before him, in haste, to carry the news of their success to their master.

God, who sees every thought, and at every moment, in every heart, saw that it was Balaam's desire to curse his Israel, and he was angry with him. And, lest he should forget his charge to him not to say any thing but what he bade him, he sent an angel with a drawn sword in his hand to stop him on his journey, and to repeat it. But Balaam's eyes were at first blinded, that he did not see him; this was the case with the eyes of Elisha's servant, who, though he saw the Syrian soldiers who had come to take his master, yet he did not see " the chariots of fire, and the horses of fire," which God had sent for his defence.

And the ass on which the prophet rode beheld the angel in the way, and she turned aside into the field: still the angel went before, and again stood still in a path of the vineyards, where there was a wall on either side; and the ass crushed her master's foot against the wall, and so got by. But the angel took another stand, where nothing could get by on the right hand or the left; and the poor animal then fell down on the ground. Balaam had beat her with his staff before, but now he beat her without mercy; and wished that he had a sword that he might kill her instantly on the spot. And God opened the mouth of the ass to reprove and to rebuke him for his cruelty. God can open or shut the mouth of any man or beast as he pleases. He could make the very stones cry out and rebuke his enemies, Luke xix. 40.

If God were now to suffer the mouths of the ox,

or the ass, or the horse, to be opened, of what
dreadful usage would many of them accuse their
owners! But, though they do not do so, a day
will come when God will ask the question which
the angel asked Balaam, Why hast thou smitten
and ill treated thy beast, — and " these three
times?" God is displeased when any one is cruel
to an insect or a brute, for his sport, or in his
anger.'

At length the Lord opened,—or took the veil
off,—from Balaam's eyes; and he saw the angel
of the Lord standing in the way, and he fell on his
face on the ground: and he said he had sinned,
and offered to go back again to his home. He was
not, however, turned from his purpose of cursing
God's people, and of getting large gain from Balak,
for the angel did not prevent his going forward;
but he charged him, at his peril, not to say any
thing but what God should bid him: and, no
doubt, the angel met him for this purpose. God
gives sinners warning after warning, that if they
will sin, they may be without excuse.'

When Balak heard that the prophet was come, he was so glad, that he went out to the very border of his land, to meet him, and to do him honour: and Balaam told him, that he was very willing to serve him,—that is, to curse Israel, but that he could not do it without God's leave; for which, no doubt, he was very sorry. Still the king was not without hope; and he offered oxen and sheep to his idol god Baal; and made a great feast for the princes of the land: and so he had done every thing, as he thought, to ensure success. What became of his vain hopes we shall hear very shortly.

QUESTIONS.

1. What cannot the curse of a wicked man do?
2. Who was cast into hell for his covetousness?
3. Of what are we in danger, if we do not resist sin at once?
4. What shall we do, if we feel as we ought, though much gain may be offered to us?
5. How must men be now judged?
6. What cannot any wicked man do?
7. When is God displeased?
8. Why does God give sinners warning upon warning?

STORY XI.

---❋---

THE KING AND THE FALSE PROPHET.

PART II.

BALAK was so rejoiced that Balaam was come, that he could scarcely close his eyes all night; he arose early in the morning, and took him to the tops of the mountains on which he used to worship idol gods; and from whence he could see the whole camp of the people whom he wished him to curse.

And Balak, at the desire of the wicked prophet, built seven altars, and offered a bullock and a ram on each. While these victims were burning, Balaam bade the king stand by them, whilst he went into a grove, or a private place, where he thought he should be more likely to meet with God.

So God met Balaam. But how did he meet with him? Did he see him in his glory, amidst a blaze of light, as when he came down on mount Sinai? No; how then? No one can tell. Perhaps, amidst the deep silence, a voice was heard, telling him what he should say. Or, rather, God might impress his word strongly on his mind without any audible voice.

In some way he knew that God was present; and Balaam said, "I have prepared seven altars, and I have offered upon every altar a bullock and a ram!" See, how he boasted, like the proud Pharisee, of his fine deeds: as if he had given God, or could give him, any thing that was not his own! As if he had now so made the Almighty his debtor, and had so obliged him, that, of course, he must give him leave, as a suitable return, to curse his people! Proud and wicked men think they have done mighty things, when they give a mere pittance of God's bounty to his poor people, or for the support of his cause;[1] but they who feel as they ought when they give, and very largely, of their gold or silver, or substance, boast not of their offerings, but say, " Of thy own give we thee!"² "We are but unprofitable servants!"

When Balaam came back, he found the king and the princes of Moab waiting for him by the altars: and now he expected that he would curse Israel. But God had put a very different word into his mouth, and, however he might wish it, he was quite unable to say any thing else. " How," said he, " shall I curse whom God hath not cursed? Or, how shall I defy whom the Lord hath not defied? For from the top of the rocks I see him, and from the hills I behold him: lo, the people shall dwell alone, and shall not be reckoned among the nations. Who can count the dust of Jacob, and the number of the fourth part of Israel? Let me die the death of the righteous; and let my last end be like his!"³

God has ever had a people in the world: and who are they? All whose hearts are created anew by his Holy Spirit; all who love to pray to him from the heart; all who repent of their sins, and

forsake them in the strength of divine grace ; and
all who fly by faith for pardon and righteousness,
to his merit, who was the great sin-offering,—who
" was wounded for our transgressions, and bruised
for our iniquities,"—all these people are, indeed,
the people of God.⁴

And though many may be inclined to curse
them, no one can really do it.　Not that their sins
did not deserve God's anger; but his dear Son has
borne that wrath which was due to them ; and has
" redeemed them from the curse of the law,"
having become himself a curse for them.⁵　So that
they are now blessed; yea, and in spite of the
utmost malice of their foes, they shall be blessed.
Neither the powers of earth or hell " shall separate them from the love of God which is in Christ
Jesus our Lord."

These people " dwell alone."　They cannot be
happy with ungodly men.　They are the friends
of all who love and serve God; and they keep company with them.　They form one blessed family,
in which they will abide for ever.　The members

of this household love one another. They " bear
one another's burdens," they "weep with each other
when they weep, and rejoice with each other when
they rejoice."⁴ They are, a blessed people: and
do I belong to them?

This family is scattered among all people, and
though there may not be many in one place, yet it
is a large one: and their number shall be as the
dew-drops of the morning. For the people shall
be willing to serve the Saviour " in the day of his
power,"—and the kingdoms of the world shall
become " the kingdoms of our God and of his
Christ."

The children of this family are so happy when
they die, that even Balaam wished to die their
death. But none can die the death of the Christian, unless they live his life: and if we think as
we ought, we shall desire as much to live his life,
as to die his death.' O Lord, I pray thee by thy
grace, to make me thy child, and to own me as
thine, living, and dying, and for ever.

So Balak was not at all pleased that Balaam

should do nothing but bless the people, when he sent for him to curse them. And he took him into another place, and again made the same offerings. From this spot, the king knew that he could see only a part of the camp of Israel; he thought now he should gain his end, as a sight of the whole put a dread of them on the spirit of the prophet. How earnest the enemies of God's people are to curse them; and how earnestly ought we to seek their good, and to pray for blessings on them.'

And God put a word into the mouth of Balaam, as he had done before; but it was very far from being such as would please Balak. "God," said he, "is not a man that he should lie, neither the son of man that he should repent: hath he said, and shall he not make it good? Behold, I have received commandment to bless; and he hath blessed, and I cannot reverse it. He hath not beheld iniquity in Jacob, neither hath he seen per- verseness in Israel: the Lord his God is with him, and the shout of a king is among them."'

How foolish it was in this king and his prophet

to think that God was like men, and would change his mind, and break his promises as readily as they do :

> " As well might he his being quit,
> As break his oath, or word forget !" [10]

How foolish it was for them to suppose, that because they made offerings to him on different places, that, therefore, he might be induced to curse his people. How true is it, that the sinner thinks God to be such an one as himself. What pride, what ignorance, and what depravity!

God will never curse his people. He does not behold any iniquity in them, on account of which he will condemn them. It is true, they have broken his holy law, and deserve his anger. But the great Redeemer has borne their sorrows, and carried their griefs. He has borne the curse so justly due to them, in his own body, on the cross. So that God does not impute sin to them, or bring it forward to their charge. He says to each of those who rest by faith on the merits of the Lord Jesus, " I am he that blotteth out thy transgressions as a cloud, and thy iniquities as a thick cloud."[11]

God is ever in the midst of his people, and they rejoice in him as their almighty and all-gracious King. Yea, they shout for joy in his presence, as loyal subjects do when their sovereign deigns to come among them:—

> " O may I hear their tribes rejoice,
>   And aid my triumphs with their voice !
>   This is my glory, Lord, to be
>   Join'd to thy saints, and near to thee !"[12]

Balaam added, " God brought them out of Egypt; he hath the strength of an unicorn. Surely there is no enchantment against Jacob, neither is there any divination against Israel: according to this time it shall be said of Jacob and of Israel, What hath God wrought! Behold, the people shall rise up as a great lion, and shall not lie down, until he eat of the prey, and drink the blood of the slain !"

But what did he mean? No doubt he meant, that as God had brought the people out of Egypt, and as Pharaoh could not prevail against them, so no other king should; that so many triumphs still awaited them, that their foes should be utterly vanquished; and that all the nations beholding these wonders, should admire, and say, " What hath God wrought!"

And all God's praying Israel, in every age, have reason to utter the same language. Let his holy name be praised, they may say, for he hath called us by his grace, and made us his children; and given us a hope full of immortality!"[13]

> " What hath God wrought! O blissful theme,
> Are we redeem'd and call'd by him?
> Shall we be led the desert through,
> And safe arrive at glory too?
>
> The news shall every harp employ;
> Fill every tongue with rapt'rous joy;
> Our souls the pleasant theme prolong,
> Then rise to join the angelic song!"[14]

H

QUESTIONS.

1. What do proud people think when they have given a little alms?

2. What do the Lord's people say when they have done all they can for his glory?

3. What word did the Lord put into Balaam's mouth?

4. Who are the people of God?

5. How are these people saved from the curse of God's holy law?

6. How do the members of God's family act towards each other?

7. If we think as we ought, what shall we do?

8. What ought we to do to God's people?

9. What was the word which God put another time into Balaam's mouth?

10. What might God as soon do, as be unfaithful?

11. What does God say to those who rest by faith on the merits of Christ for salvation?

12. What is our glory?

13. What may God's people say?

14. Repeat the lines at the close of the story.

STORY XII.

—✼—

THE KING AND THE FALSE PROPHET.

PART III.

BALAK vainly thought that his gods were more likely to hear if prayers were offered from some spot more valued by them than another. So he took Balaam to one from which he had the most hope. There he built altars, and killed and burnt bullocks and rams as he had done before.

But Balaam did not go out into a secret place as he had at other times; he set his face towards the wilderness, in which the people of Israel pitched their camp. And now the Spirit of God took hold of him in such a way, that he was compelled to speak as he bade him. So he said, "How goodly are thy tents, O Jacob; and thy tabernacles, O Israel!" They whose eyes are

H 2

indeed opened by God's Spirit, see that God's servants, though they may dwell in tents, and be ever so poor, are " the excellent of the earth;"[1] and they will delight in their converse and friendship.

And then Balaam compared the people of Israel to gardens by the river side, which are very fruitful; and to beautiful cedar trees which the Lord hath planted. He said, that, so far from being a cursed people, their affairs should flourish, and their king should be of greater dignity than the highest sovereign among the other nations. He again reminded Balak of the wonderful manner in which God had brought them out of Egypt, and told him that he would still bless them, and crown them with victory over their enemies; so that they should spoil them, as easily as a strong lion rends and devours his prey. And he closed his speech, crying out aloud, " Blessed is he that blesseth thee; and cursed is he that curseth thee!"[2] This was no better than cursing Balak; and no wonder that he was so very far from being pleased.

He was, indeed, very angry; and he smote his

hands together. " I called thee," said he, " to curse my enemies; and, behold, thou hast altogether blessed them these three times. Therefore, now, flee thou to thy place; I thought to promote thee unto great honour; but, lo, the Lord hath kept thee back from honour."

But Balaam said, " Spake I not also to thy messengers which thou sentest me, saying, If Balak would give me his house full of silver and gold, I cannot go beyond the commandment of the Lord; but what the Lord said, that will I speak."

Balak said falsely, that the Lord had kept Balaam back from honour, because he would not permit him to curse his people,—for there can be no real honour in breaking any of the commands of God.' Sin is the transgression of the law. Is it not shameful to disobey a good and kind parent? It is. And how much more shameful, then, must it be to offend God! Is it not shameful to steal, and curse, and not to love God? It is. Then all sin is shameful. Living and dying in sin, we shall awake " to shame and everlasting contempt."'

Before this false prophet went home, he told Balak some of those things which should happen in the history of the people whom he wished to be cursed. " There shall come," said he, " a Star out of Jacob, and a Sceptre shall arise out of Israel; and he shall have dominion."

The great Redeemer was, no doubt, referred to by the Star which should arise out of Israel; though Balaam did not understand the language which he was uttering. So Caiaphas the high priest prophesied, that one man, even Jesus, should die for the people;* but he did not know fully what he said.

The great Deliverer is called a star to denote his glory. For he is the " King of kings, and Lord of lords." Think of the names he bears,—he is " the Wonderful, Counsellor, the Mighty God, the everlasting Father, the Prince of Peace."⁵ Think of what he has done: the stormy seas heard his word, and became calm; the helpless paralytic arose at his bidding, took up his bed, and carried it home.⁶

---

* John xi. 51.

At his command, the tongue of the dumb was unloosed, and sang his praises.⁶ The devils fled at his rebuke. Even the dead heard his voice, and came from the tomb.⁶ Yea, " he was in the world, and the world was made by him, and the world knew him not."⁶ And there is one work which he has done mightier than all these,—he bare the wrath of God, so justly due to the sins of all who fly to him for salvation; no created being, however high, could have done this:

" 'Twas great to speak a world from nought;
'Twas greater to redeem !"⁶

By the " sceptre," which it is said he shall hold, is meant his authority and dominion; for " of his kingdom there shall be no end." " His dominion is an everlasting dominion, which shall not pass away, and his kingdom that which shall not be destroyed."⁷ " His name shall endure for ever; his name shall be continued as long as the sun, and men shall be blessed in him; all nations shall call him blessed."⁸ I pray thee, O Lord, to make me one of his happy subjects.

This wicked prophet said, he should see the great Redeemer, " but not nigh." This looks as if he foretold his own wretched state. For there is reason to think, that Balaam lived and died in his sins, as he was slain when fighting against the very people whom he wished to curse.⁹ It is an awful thought, that a man may have the gifts of an angel, and yet finally perish.¹⁰ He may sometimes faintly wish, to " die the death of the righteous," yet go on in sin, die the death of the wicked, and be lost for ever.

QUESTIONS.

1. What do they see whose eyes are opened by God's Spirit ?
2. What did Balaam say of God's people ?
3. In what is there no real honour ?
4. What will be our state, if we live and die in sin ?
5. What are the names which the Redeemer bears ?
6. Mention some of the works which the Redeemer has wrought ?
7. What kind of dominion is that of the Lord Jesus ?
8. Who shall be blessed in Christ ?
9. How did Balaam live and die ?
10. What is an awful thought ?

STORY XIII.

—❋—

RAHAB AND THE SPIES.

THE people of the land of Canaan had become so very vile, that the cry of their sins came up before God; and he was so angry, that he told Joshua to cut them off, and to take the country.

As he was now coming near one of the cities of the land called Jericho, he sent two young men to see how things were, and how he had best attack it.

Now there was a woman whose name was Rahab, who had a house which was on the wall of the town, where it is supposed she used to lodge and entertain strangers and travellers.

It seems very likely, that she had often heard from the people who came to her house, how the Lord had brought Israel out of Egypt, and how he had fought on their side, and given many kings and people into their hand. So that these things were spread abroad among the people of Jericho; and the king heard of them, and he and his subjects were much afraid lest the city should be destroyed. And the Lord had told Rahab, in some way, that this would be the case.

Now there were strong and high walls around Jericho, and the king had set a watch about the gates, that he might know who went out and came in.

And the spies came in at the gate, as secretly as they could, and they went to the house of Rahab, who received them, though she knew for what they had come, with much kindness.

Once she had been a wicked woman, but by God's mercy and grace, she was turned from the error of her ways. For it is said, it was by faith in God's word, that he would bless his people, and punish their foes, she took in the spies sent by Joshua. And all must be turned from their sins by the power of God's Spirit, or they cannot belong to God's people, nor can they, at last, enter into heaven.[1]

And though the men came in, perhaps, one at a

time, and very silently, at the gate of the town, and went to the house of Rahab, the king soon knew all about it, and he sent a message to her; " Bring forth," said he, " the men that are come to thee; for they be come to search out the country."

Before the king's servants came, she had heard of their errand; and she took the spies up to the roof of her house, which was flat, as the roofs of dwellings in the east still are: here she had a large quantity of stalks of flax, which were drying in the sun; and with these she hid the young men.

Then she went down, and the king's servants came, and told their message. And she said, " There came men to me, but I wist not whence they were. About the time of the shutting of the gate, they went out; whither they went, I wot not,—pursue after them quickly, for ye shall overtake them." And they did so, but they could not find them; for they were under the stalks of flax on the roof of her house.

When the king's officers were gone, she went up to the men, and said, " I know that the Lord hath given you the land, and that the terror of you has fallen upon us, and all the inhabitants of the land faint because of you. For we have heard how the Lord dried up the waters of the Red Sea for you, when you came out of Egypt;" and what you did to the giant kings, Sihon and Og, whom " ye utterly destroyed." When we heard these things, there remained no more courage in any man among us; for the Lord your God, " he is God in heaven above, and in the earth beneath."

And then she prayed them to spare her life, and the lives of her kindred, when they should take and destroy this city. And they solemnly engaged to do so.

Now, as her house was upon the town wall, she told them, that she would let them down with the scarlet line she had in her hand from her window.

That they might know the house again, it was agreed between them, that she should bind this scarlet line, so as it might be easily seen, on her casement. And when she had let them down, she did so in their sight.

Before they went away, she advised them not to go in the direct road to the fords of Jordan, but to go round by the mountains, that they might not meet the king's messengers. And they did so, and escaped, and came safely to Joshua, and told him all that had happened to them.

But was it right for Rahab to tell the king's servants, that she did not know who the men were, though it is plain she did? And that they were gone, when she knew they were on the top of her house covered with the stalks of flax? It was not right. The plain command of God is, that no one must on any account tell a lie.' Though her design was good, no doubt she committed sin.

See how full of fear she was, lest she should be cut off with the wicked people of the city by God's judgments, and how carefully she sought after deliverance. She felt as Noah did, who, "moved with fear, built an ark, to the saving of his house; by the which he condemned the world, and became heir of the righteousness which is by faith." And ought not every one to be afraid, lest God shoul .

call him into judgment for his sins?[3] "The wages of sin is death;" and if we receive the wages due to our sins, we are undone for ever.[4] How, then, ought each of us, and without delay, to flee from "the wrath to come."

Rahab was not only concerned for her own deliverance, but for that of her father, and mother, and of all her kindred. In like manner, we should not be satisfied with a good hope of our own salvation, but we should pray and strive all we can, to take our parents and children, and all that belong to us, to "the city that hath foundations, whose maker and builder is God."[5]

QUESTIONS.

1. What must every one be, if they would be among God's people and enter heaven?

2. What is the plain command of God?

3. What will be our state if we receive the wages due to our sins?

5. For what should we pray and strive?

JERICHO.

STORY XIV.

JERICHO.

Now Jericho was a strong city, full of fighting men, and the walls of it were very high. The gates also were kept shut night and day; no one went out, or came in.

Joshua might fear, on these accounts, that he should have much trouble to take the city. But as he came to look at it, and was thinking what method it would be best to pursue, the Lord appeared to him, in the form of a man, and told him to take courage, as he had come as the Leader of the people. "See," said he, "I have given Jericho into thy hand!"

"*Have* given,"—why, the people had not yet come near the walls? how was this? God often

speaks in his word of things which he proposes to
do, as if they were already done.   For who can
prevent the Almighty from doing as he pleases ?
His words are works.

Now the Lord, who had appeared to him, told
him what they should do.   They were not to beat
the walls with heavy instruments, till they had
broken a part of them down, and so go in through
the breach ; nor were they to burn the gates, or
get into the city by means of ladders ; for the city
was to be taken as no place was ever taken before
or since.   " Ye shall compass the city," said he,
" all ye men of war; and go round about the city
once : thus shalt thou do for six days.   And seven
priests shall bear before the ark seven trumpets of
rams' horns : and the seventh day ye shall compass
the city seven times, and the priests shall blow
with the trumpets.   And it shall come to pass,
that when they make a long blast with the rams'
horns, and when ye hear the sound of the trumpet,
all the people shall shout with a great shout :
and the wall of the city shall fall down flat,

and the people shall ascend up every man straight before him!"

What a strange way was this in which to take a town. It would not have been wonderful if the people had said, How can this be! Who ever heard of a town having been taken in this way? Of what use can it be to shout? How can strong walls be brought down with a shout! Let us attack the city with our weapons, and then there will be some hope of our gaining it! But God told them to walk round it, and shout, to show that he could give them victory, and bring about his designs, with or without means, and as he pleased, to teach them to trust in him at all times, and in all places.'

And Joshua and the people did as the Lord bade them; they marched round the city once a day, for six days, in solemn silence; and no sound was heard but that of the rams' horns, which the priests blew.

But why did not the walls fall down the first time when the people marched round them?

I

Because it was the will of God that they should
not. By keeping them for seven days in their
movement round the place, the Lord meant to
give them so much time to observe and to think
of God's wonderful works, that they should never
forget them;[3] and, perhaps, he meant to show
them, that they should exactly obey his commands,
though they might not fully understand the reason
of them, and without asking any questions.[4]

But how was it that they were to take the city
on the sabbath-day? Had not God said in his
law, that they were not to do any work on this
holy day? Yes: but God may, if he pleases, for
a season, dispense with his own laws; no other
being, however, must dare to do so. The poor
blind man, to whom our Lord gave eyes, was right,
when he told the Pharisees, who found fault with
him for carrying his bed on the sabbath-day, that
he who had given him eyes, was, no doubt, a
Divine person, as no other could have done this;
and he said to him, "Take up thy bed, and go to
thy house."

But how was it that the people of the city, when they saw the priests, and the army, going their rounds, did not shoot darts, or cast stones, and kill them? Most likely, they were so far from the walls, that they were unable to reach them. Many of the people did, no doubt, look at this odd sort of parade, as they would term it, and would scoff, and treat them with contempt. And as they saw them march round day after day, and no harm come to the city, they began to think they were very safe; and that neither Israel, nor Israel's God, could do them any injury.

If they did think so, they did not think right; for on the sabbath-day morning, the people rose early, and marched round the city seven times. What a moment that must have been when they all stood still, and fixed their eyes on the walls of the city! When the priests blew with their trumpets, and Joshua said to the people, " Shout! for the Lord hath given you this city."

" So the people shouted, when the priests blew with the trumpets; and it came to pass, when the

I 2

people heard the sound of the trumpets, that the people shouted with a great shout, and the wall fell down flat, so that the people went up into the city, every man straight before him; and they took the city."

But Joshua had told the people the command of God, since the city had made itself so hateful in his sight, on account of its wickedness, that every living thing must be destroyed; but the gold and silver, brass and iron, were to be devoted to the service of the Lord; only Rahab and her kindred were to be preserved, according to the covenant made with the spies. And these young men sought out and saved them; indeed, they were all in one house, in the window of which the scarlet line was bound.

When the men of the city saw the walls fall down at once with a dreadful crash, they were struck with terror, and had no strength, or even desire, to resist, and so they became an easy prey. And Joshua destroyed the city, and laid it waste, as God had charged him.

God has a right to cut off, and he can do it in an instant, any one who dares rebel against him. And if there be a town, or even a world full of rebels, he has a right to punish, or to consume the whole.

But would it be right for one people now to go and take the city of another nation, and to destroy it? No; unless, indeed, God had given them, as he gave to his servant Joshua, an express command to do so.

And God gave the people the city by the sounding of the rams' horns, and the shouting of the people, to convince us, that in every age he can fulfil his mightiest purposes by the feeblest means.[5] It was his design to feed vast multitudes of people during a dreadful famine of seven years; and he did so by means of a Hebrew youth who was sold for a slave.[6] It was his design that the Gospel should be preached, and the kingdom of the Saviour set up among the nations; and he has done it, by a small company of fishermen, tent-makers, and carpenters. And why? That " no flesh might glory in his presence; but, as it is written, Let him that glorieth, glory only in the Lord!"

QUESTIONS.

1. What were the people to do on the seventh day after going round Jericho?

2. Why did God bid the people walk round the city and shout, that the walls might fall down?

3. Why were the people to march round the city for seven days?

4. Give me another reason?

5. How can God fulfil his mightiest purposes?

6. Give me two instances in which he has done so.

STORY XV.

—❋—

THE PRAYING YOUTH.

THE name of this youth was Samuel. He had a very kind and pious mother. She prayed for him very often, and the Lord heard her prayer.

When he was yet but a child, she brought him into the temple, and he worshipped the Lord there. It must have been a fine sight to have beheld him lifting up his little hand, and asking God to bless him. There are still very many dear children and youth who call on God, as Samuel did. Each should ask himself, Do I do so? Happy is the child who can say, I do; and, by God's grace, I ever will:[1]

> " My heart resolves, my tongue obeys,
>   And angels shall rejoice:
> To hear their mighty Maker's praise
>   Sound from a feeble voice."

Samuel was under the care of Eli, the High Priest; and there was a little room near the temple in which he slept. Now one evening, when he had prayed God to bless him, he laid down to rest. But before sunrise, when the light in the golden lamp used to be put out, Samuel was awake, and he heard a voice, and it said, " Samuel !" So he thought that Eli called him; and he got up and went to him. When parents or friends call us, we should go to them as soon as we can.

Eli bade him go and lie down again, as he did not call him; and he did so. And he heard the same voice call him again and again, and he went to Eli; and Eli saw that the Lord had called him; and he said, Go and lie down again, and when you shall hear the voice, say, " Speak, Lord, for thy servant heareth;" and he did so,—and the Lord sent him with a message to Eli.

And does God ever call to youth now? Yes. How I should like to hear his voice! Should you? Then you may, if you will but listen. God has put something within every person which tells him when he does good or bad.' When you have got up in the morning, or laid down in the evening, and have not thanked God for his goodness, nor asked God to bless you; when you have not minded what your parents and teachers said; when you have spoken bad words, or what was not true;' did not something within you say, you had done wrong? Well, that was the voice of God, and it called to you.

Perhaps your dear father or mother has died, and they were taken from their home, and laid in the cold grave. That was God's voice to you; and it said, My dear youth, will you not now cry unto me, My Father! be thou the guide of my youth.'

You read in the Bible, that unless the heart is changed by God's Holy Spirit, and made sorry for its sins; and unless we trust alone in the merits of the Lord Jesus, and love and serve him, we shall be lost;' now this is God's voice speaking to every one, and it says, Henry, William, Mary, or Ann, —or whatever their names may be,—you will be lost, unless you are sorry for your sins; and trust in, and love, and serve the Lord Jesus. And are you doing so?

We should pray for grace, that we may hear, and mind the call of God to-day; we are not certain that we may be spared to hear him calling to us to-morrow.

If we do, indeed, wish to meet with God, we should go alone, and think of him, and lift up our heart to him, and say, O Lord, I beseech thee, for Christ's sake, come and bless and save me.[6] He has said in his holy word, "Draw nigh unto me, and I will draw nigh unto you;" and we are sure that he will fulfil his promises.

He knows when we go to some secret place to pray to him, and to praise him. When Nathaniel went under the shade of the fig-tree to do so, his eye was on him for good; and he is the same now as he was then.[7]

When you go into the house of God on the Lord's day, you should say, "Speak, Lord, for thy servant heareth!" Bless thy holy word, which I am about to hear, for the good of my soul, both in this world, and in that which is to come.[8]

When you open the blessed Bible, you should lift up your heart to God, and say, " Speak, Lord, for thy servant heareth !" Let me not read it in vain. " Open thou mine eyes, that I may behold wondrous things out of thy law." Write its great truths, I pray thee, by thy Spirit, on my memory and on my heart.[9]

When you kneel down to pray, then say, " Speak, Lord, for thy servant heareth !" Teach me to know, and help me to do, all thy holy will. So I shall be a child of thine, and be owned and blessed by thee for ever.[10]

QUESTIONS.

1. Who is the happy child ?

2. What has God put within every one ?

3. Mention the times when conscience has told you that you have done wrong.

4. What did God's voice say to you when you lost dear parents ?

5. What does God's voice say to us in his holy word ?

6. What should we do if we indeed wish to meet with God ?

7. What did Nathaniel do ?

8. What should we say, when we go into the house of God ?

9. What should we say, when we open the Bible ?

10. And when we kneel down to pray ?

THE ARK AND DAGON.

STORY XVI.

—✳—

THE ARK AND DAGON.

THE sons of Eli, the High Priest, were very wicked, and they led the people to attack the Philistines, a nation that lived near them; and the men of Israel were smitten, so that four thousand of them were left dead on the field of battle.

In this trouble, they began to ask, what they should do. And they thought they would take the Ark of God, and go and fight their enemies again: vainly supposing, that the Lord would be sure now to appear for them and give them victory.

And when the Ark of God was brought into the camp, the people "shouted with a great shout, so that the very earth rang again." And when their foes heard this shout, and knew on what account it was, they were greatly afraid, and said, Their God is come up among them; woe unto us! Who shall deliver us out of the hand of this mighty God, who smote the Egyptians?"

Now the Ark of God was a coffer, made of beautiful wood, and spread over with gold within and without. In it, among other sacred things, were the tables of God's covenant with the people. The lid of it was solid gold; and was called the mercy-seat,—for from above this, out of a cloud, God often, in great mercy, made his will known to his servants.

God never meant that this Ark should be taken out to the field of battle. And the Ark, without the blessing of the God of the Ark, could do them no good; and so they found it. Israel was beaten again; many thousands were slain; the Ark of God fell into the hand of the Philistines; the sons of Eli were cut off; and Eli himself dropped down and died when he heard of the loss of the Ark.

The Philistines now thought that their god Dagon, which was nothing but a senseless image, the upper half in the form of a man, and the lower, in that of a fish, was far greater than the God of Israel. So, in contempt of God, and in honour of Dagon, they brought the Ark into the house of Dagon, and set it by Dagon, and, no doubt, they praised their god as a very fine god.

This wretched image, which they served and prayed to as their god, could not even stand of itself; so it was " fastened up with nails," Isa. xli. 7. What a poor god, that could not so much as stand, without being held up with props and spikes!

But when the priests went in the morning into the temple, " behold Dagon was fallen on his face to the earth before the Ark of the Lord." So they were very sad, and they took up their poor god, and nailed him to the wall faster than before, and thus he stood up for that day.

But the next morning, in spite of all their care, they found Dagon in a worse plight still; for he had fallen upon his face upon the ground before the Ark of the Lord; and his head, and the palms of his hands, were cut off upon the threshold, only the stump, or fishy part of Dagon was left." All the attempts of the greatest or the richest to set up any religion or worship, but that which God has made known in his word, is only like setting up Dagon.[2] It is but a vain effort to raise and to prop up that which the Almighty God has said he will cast down. The empire of Satan shall as surely fall before the kingdom of Christ, as Dagon fell before the Ark.[3]

As the people had despised the Ark, and the God of the Ark, and cried up their god Dagon, God taught them better by his judgments. He troubled the people of the city with a painful disease; so that the cry of their torment went up to the heavens.

Now they began to fear that they suffered thus on account of the dishonour put on the Ark of God. So they sent it to another city called Gath. There the judgment of God fell upon the people, and they would not permit the Ark to stay. So they sent it to Ekron; and the people of this place sent it on to another. And so, for seven months, they kept removing it; but God's anger every where fell upon the people, and none of them were at last willing to receive the Ark. They who contemn God, and harden themselves against him, can never prosper.

Still they were unwilling to send back the Ark. Their having it, they thought a proof of the power of their great god Dagon. At last, however, as the cities would not receive it, they put it out into the open field. They thought no harm could come to them by its being there. But God sent large multitudes of mice, which ate up all their corn. See how God can bring down and humble his proudest foes by things that are utterly despised,—by mice, or flies, or frogs, or locusts.[5] Thus trouble after trouble came on them, till they had really sent back the Ark. The way to get rid of our troubles, is to pray, in good earnest, for grace to part with our sins.[6]

So they consulted their priests; and they told them that they could not prevail against the God

who had brought his people out of Egypt, " with
a high hand." They advised them to send back
the Ark; and to make figures of gold of the disease with which they had been punished, and of
the mice that had devoured their harvests. Thus
confessing, how the god of the Ark had visited
them, and owning his power and glory, and their
own disgrace.' And they sent these, with the
Ark, into the land of Israel. See, God himself,
without any help of the people, brought back
the Ark. What is there which is too hard for
the Lord? Is there any god like the God of
Israel?

But the way in which the Ark was taken back
was wonderful. The people took two milch-kine,
tied them to a new cart, and shut up their calves
at home. And they laid the Ark of the Lord upon
the cart, and the coffer with the mice of gold, and
the images of their disease.'

And God so ordered it that the kine not only
left their calves, but took the direct road,—for
they had no driver, or guide,—to the first town of

the land of Israel, which was a distance of about
eight or nine miles.

The kine went on, lowing for their calves, but
did not turn back, or turn aside to graze in the
fields, to the right hand or the left. God, by his
providence, overrules the course of the brute creation as he pleases, for his own glory. " The ox
knoweth his owner, and the ass his master's crib;"
though men, who are called rational, are unmindful
of the hand that formed, and which sustains them
every moment.

No doubt the lords of the Philistines, and the
priests of Dagon, followed the Ark at a distance;
because they said, We will see if the kine go up
by the plain road to Bethshemesh, a city of Israel,
when we will conclude, that the God of the Ark
has troubled and punished us; but if they will not
advance in that way, but turn back to their calves,
we will conclude that it is not he, but " a chance
that has happened to us;" as if there could be
any chance in God's dominion, without " whom a
sparrow does not fall to the ground."

When they saw the kine move in a direct line to the land of Israel, they were, no doubt, filled with wonder at the manifold proofs of the presence and power of the God of Israel.'

" And the people of Bethshemesh," whither the kine brought the Ark, " were reaping their wheat-harvest in the valley ; and they lifted up their eyes, and saw the Ark, and rejoiced to see it." And there was a great stone there, and on this they placed the Ark.

Then they brake up the cart for fuel for God's altar, that it might not be used for any common purpose ; and, on the same account, they offered the kine as " a burnt-offering unto the Lord."

But what became of Dagon ? Did they fasten on his head and hands again, and once more fix him up with nails as their god ? Or did they get some plaster, and make a new god ? They were so foolish, and depraved, that most likely they did either the one or the other.

The Lord, the God of Irael, he is the living and the true God. His smile is life, and his frown is death. He alone hath made the heavens and the earth, the sea and the dry land. " He is our God; and we are the people of his pasture, and the sheep of his hand. He is a great God, and a great king above all gods. O come, let us worship and bow down; let us kneel before the Lord our Maker." [16]

~~~~~~~~~~~~~~~~

QUESTIONS.

1. Why was the lid of the Ark called the Mercy-seat?
2. What is setting up false religion like?
3. What is a vain effort?
4. What shall surely fall?
5. How can God bring down the proudest of his foes?
6. What is the best way to get rid of our troubles?
7. What did the Philistines confess by sending back the Ark with the images of gold?
8. How was the Ark brought back into the land of Israel?
9. What did the movement of the kine prove?
10. Repeat the paragraph which ends the story.

STORY XVII.

—✳—

THE CHILD OF DAVID.

KING DAVID greatly sinned against the Lord, and the Lord said he would punish him for his sin; and he did so in several ways. He afflicted, and took away a child who was very dear to him; and, no doubt, for wise ends; he has good reasons for his conduct, whether we may see them or not.

Besides, we are sure that nothing can happen by chance: we are told in the Bible, that "troubles do not spring out of the ground;" and that " a sparrow does not fall" without our heavenly Father. So, we are sure, the Lord's hand was to be seen in the illness of the child of the king. And, if we do indeed love him, he will change our sorrows into blessings.[1]

Joseph saw God's hand in the events of his life. "It was not you who sent me into Egypt," said he to his brethren," but God, to save much people alive." The Sabeans and Chaldeans took away Job's cattle; but he said, "The Lord gave, and the Lord hath taken away, blessed be the name of the Lord!"

Sin and suffering are always found together. How is it, then, that a babe, who has never sinned, becomes ill, and suffers, and dies? Is not God wise, and good, and just, and gracious? How, then, can these things be? Can God be less good and kind than an earthly parent? Surely not.

No one can answer these questions without the Bible. There we learn, that, as all are the children of Adam, all are sinful,—even the little babe; for who can bring a clean thing out of an unclean? No, not one." Hence it is, that even children suffer and die;

> "They die, for Adam sinned: they live, for Christ has
> died." [2]

" By one man sin entered into the world, and

death by sin; and so death passed upon all, for
that all have sinned."³   But no one was ever lost,
except on account of his own sins.

The child of the king was taken very ill; and he
was much troubled; and betook himself to earnest
prayer.   He knew that prayer had moved, and
that it does move the hand which moves the world.⁴
He knew, that in answer to his own prayers, God
had often been better to him than all his fears;
and so, as he had found help from prayer, he
prayed; and he humbled himself for his sin.   And
he said, " I acknowledge my transgression.   Have
mercy upon me, O God.   Make me to hear joy
and gladness, that the bones which thou hast broken
may rejoice."⁵

Pardon of sin is always connected with true repentance.   And God never forgives any one who
is not really sorry for his sins, and who does not
forsake them;⁶ this was the case with David, and
God forgave his sins, but he did not answer his
prayer in sparing the life of the child.

For though he fasted, and would not sit down

with his family to eat bread, and lay all night upon the earth, and earnestly besought the Lord to restore the child, yet he grew worse; and on the seventh day from the beginning of his illness, he died.

And now the servants of the king did not know what to do. They feared to tell their master these sad tidings; they said, " Behold, while the child was yet alive, we spake unto him, and he would not hearken to our voice; how will he then vex himself, if we tell him that the child is dead?" But from the " whisperings," of his servants, the king thought what had happened; and he asked, and they said, " He is dead!"

" Then David arose from the earth, and washed, and anointed himself, and changed his apparel, and came into the house of the Lord, and worshipped; and he came into his own house, and they set bread before him, and he did eat."

And his servants were so much surprised at his conduct, that some of them ventured to say to him, " What is this that thou hast done? Thou didst fast and weep for the child while it was alive, but when the child was dead, thou didst rise and eat bread." And the king replied, " While the child was yet alive, I fasted and wept; for I said, Who can tell, whether God will be gracious to me, that the child may live? But now he is dead, wherefore should I fast? Can I bring him back again? I shall go to him, but he shall not return to me."

Two things checked his grief, and made him calmly submit to the will of God. One was, that the case was decided, and could not be altered. When a dear child dies, the Divine will is as plain as if a voice from heaven had declared it : and who, then, are we, or any of our race, that we or they should dare murmur at it? We should say, as Eli did, " It is the Lord, let him do what seemeth him good!"'

The other ground of comfort was, that he should ere long go to the dear child, though he could not come back to him. What did he mean? into the grave? No, there would have been no joy in this. No doubt he believed, that the happy spirit of his dear boy had entered into heaven, where all the family of God are to dwell together for ever. And, surely, with a good hope of soon meeting our children and friends in that blessed society, we may well wipe away our tears, and say, We shall go to them, though they return not again unto us.[8]

QUESTIONS.

1. What does God do for those who love him?
2. Why do children suffer, and why are they saved?
3. How did sin and death enter into our world?
4. What has prayer done, and what does it do?
5. Repeat the expressions of David's repentance.
6. Who does God forgive?
7. What should we say when a child or friend dies?
8. What should a good hope of meeting our children and friends in heaven induce us to do and to say?

STORY XVIII.

OBADIAH.

AHAB, the king of Israel, was wicked beyond all the kings that had reigned. Among other ways by which he showed his contempt of God, he set up the idol Baal, and commanded his people to worship this image.

So God said, I'll give them no dew or rain, and let them see whether this image can pour down showers, and give fruitful seasons, or help them. And Elijah, the prophet, prayed that it might be so; not from hatred to them, but that the king and his subjects might see, that none but God could bless, or do them good.[1]

And so there was no corn to make bread, and the people were dying for want; and there was no grass or water for the cattle; and so most of them died.

This sad state of things had lasted for more than three years; and Ahab, and his wife, and subjects, were no better for God's judgment; they went on to worship Baal, and sought to take away the life of Elijah; but he fled, and they could not find him.

No words can describe how wretched the people were; " the vines were dried up, and the fig-trees languished; the pomegranate trees, the palm, the apple, and all the trees of the field, were withered? the fire devoured the pastures, and the flocks were desolate. The nobles sent their little ones to the waters; they came to the springs, but found none, and returned with their vessels empty. The seed rotted under the clods, the gardens were laid desolate, the barns were broken down, and the corn perished. The wild asses stood in the high places, their eyes failed, becauses there was no grass. Yea, the hind also calved in the field, and forsook it, because there was no grass." And Baal could

not give them a single blade, or one drop of rain.
God alone is the Giver, and the Father of the rain
and of the dew.[2]

The king had some horses and mules which he
much prized, and he was afraid they would die;
so he called for Obadiah, the governor of his
palace, and sent him one way through the land,
whilst he went the other, in search of grass, and
fountains of water. The king was afraid to send
any other persons, lest if they should find any they
might keep it.

Now Baal could not pity or help them, for he
was but an image that had no life, but God could,
and he did. For though, like many in our day,
Ahab had more concern about his beasts, than for
the welfare of his soul, and the glory of God, yet
the Lord sent Elijah to meet Obadiah, and to
charge him to tell the king that he was about to
" send rain upon the earth." When no one can
help us, God can;[3] and we should never despair of
seeing and enjoying his mercy.[4]

And Obadiah met the prophet; and he fell on

his face before him, and said, " Art thou my lord Elijah ?" And as Ahab wanted to find the prophet,—not for any good we may be sure,—he told Obadiah to go to him, and let him know where he was.

But he was afraid to be the bearer of such a message. For though he knew that Ahab had sent far and near in search of him; yet he thought that the king might suppose that he was a friend to the prophet, and so slay him. In what, therefore, said he, have I offended thee, that " thou shouldst deliver thy servant into the hand of Ahab ?"

And he was also afraid, that the Spirit of the Lord might take Elijah away from that place, whilst he was gone to tell the king, and so he would be angry with him, and think that he trifled with and mocked him ; perhaps something like this had taken place, to show Ahab how vain his malice was against this servant of the Lord. If God be for us, none can be against us, so as to do us any real harm.

Still Obadiah besought the prophet not to employ him on this dangerous errand; and humbly reminded him, how many of the Lord's servants would most likely be cut off if he were to perish.

Now this good man had begun to fear God, when he was yet but a youth; and

> " When we devote our youth to God,
>   'Tis pleasing in his eyes;
> A flower when offered in the bud,
>   Is no vain sacrifice."

But how did he show that he feared the Lord? No doubt, he bowed to his authority; the will of the Lord was more to him than that of all other beings united.[5] He said, as Samuel did, " Speak, Lord, for thy servant heareth !" He feared to offend God. He worshipped and served him, and he would not bow his knees to Baal.[6] He was truly religious. How wonderful it was to find such a servant of the Lord in the palace of Ahab. Good people are sometimes found where we should least expect them.

The word Obadiah means, a servant of the Lord.

And how great is the honour of being his servant, who made, and who supports, the heavens and the earth, and the boundless waters of the mighty deep! And how unspeakable is the happiness of such a relation; for he who cannot but fulfil his promise has said, " Where I am, there also shall my servant be !"'

But Obadiah feared the Lord greatly. We are sure of this, or he would not have done what he did. When Jezebel cut off all the Lord's prophets on whom she could lay her hands, this good man befriended them; for though he had not room in his house to conceal or lodge them, he had two large caves, and he fitted them up, and put fifty in each, and fed them with bread and water; which was the best provision he could get in this time of famine.*

Obadiah did not say, as we are sure many in our day would have done, What! take in fifty prophets! O no, how great a trouble it will be, and I have enough to do with my own affairs! Get bread and water for a hundred people! why what

L

an expense! it will reduce me to poverty; I cannot think of it! And then, in this time of scarcity, how do I know I shall get enough bread and water for my own household? no, they must shift as they can. And if Jezebel should know it, and most likely she will,—for how can so much provision be brought to my house without its being known,— why, then we shall all perish together. No, let them hide themselves where they may: I cannot think of having them here! Obadiah did not say any thing like this.[9]

At the judgment-day the Lord Jesus will point to his people, and say, "I was hungry, and ye gave me meat; thirsty, and ye gave me drink; sick, and in prison, and ye visited me; naked, and ye clothed me. Inasmuch as ye have done it to one of the least of these, my brethren, ye have done it unto me!"[10]

And now, to raise Obadiah above his fears, Elijah solemnly assured him that he would indeed meet the king. "As the Lord of Hosts," said he, "liveth, before whom I stand, I will surely show myself unto him to-day." And Obadiah went to find Ahab; and he came to meet Elijah. It was a wonderful meeting, as we shall find if we read the next story.

QUESTIONS.

1. What did Elijah want Ahab and his subjects to see and feel?

2. Who alone can give rain and dew?

3. Who can help us when no other can?

4. Of what should we never despair?

5. What does Dr. Watts say of our devoting our youth to God?

6. How was it evident that Obadiah feared the Lord?

7. What is the promise of the Lord to his servants?

8. What did Obadiah do for a hundred of the Lord's prophets?

9. What did Obadiah not say?

10. What will Christ say to his servants on the great day?

STORY XIX.

—✳—

ELIJAH AND THE FALSE PROPHETS.

When Obadiah saw the prophet, he bowed with his face towards the ground, and said, " Art thou my lord Elijah?" But Ahab's address was very different: " Art thou he," said he sternly, " that troubleth Israel?" We may soon know whether persons love God or not, by what they say of his people and ministers.[1]

Elijah was no enemy, but a friend to the king, and to his people; for, if they had done what he wished them, they would have been kept from those sins which had brought down the judgments of God. Wicked men cannot bear the faithful reproofs of the servants of the Lord; and, instead of being thankful, they hate and slander them.

And the prophet told Ahab plainly who it was that had troubled Israel, and brought a famine on the land. " I have not troubled Israel," said he, " but thou and thy father's house." Sin does trouble people ; it makes the man who commits it wretched ; it makes families unhappy, and nations miserable. It has brought a dreadful flood of evil upon the world.'

And Elijah talked a long while with the king. At last, that it might be seen whether he was right, or the false prophets and Ahab, he wished them to be sent for to Mount Carmel, on the top of which they now were. And Elijah proposed, that the priests of the idol Baal should build an altar, and put a quantity of wood on it, and lay a bullock, cut in pieces, upon the fuel, and that he would do the same ; and that they should cry to their god Baal, whilst he would call on the living and true God, and that the God which should answer prayer, by sending fire to burn up the bullock, should be owned as the living and true God. And Ahab sent for the false prophets.

Now there were many of the people who were
sometimes for Baal, and sometimes they spoke as
if they would serve the Lord ; they had not settled
it in their mind what they would do.   So Elijah
said to them, " How long halt ye between two
opinions ?   If the Lord be God," if he alone be
the Creator, Preserver, and Benefactor of all ; if
he alone can give rain, and fruitful seasons, why,
then, own him as such,—obey, and " follow him !"
But if Baal can do these things, then " follow
him."   They who are not with the Saviour, are
against him.⁸   Every one should say, as Joshua
did, " Choose ye whom ye will serve ; but as for
me," I have made up my mind, that " I will serve
the Lord !"⁴

Mark the courage of Elijah ; he stood alone ;
there were four hundred and fifty priests of Baal,
the king, and the queen, most of the great men,
and nearly all the people, against him.   God's
cause is not shown by the number of voices that
are lifted up on its behalf.   If it had been now
put to the vote, the idol god Baal, only fit to be

burnt, or to be cast to the dunghill, would have
been preferred to the Creator of the heavens and
the earth.⁵ .Though the multitude will not go
with us to heaven, we must not go with them to
hell. Though the great, and the rich, and the
mighty, contemn God, and refuse to obey him, we
shall perish with them if we do not love and serve
him.⁶

So, as it has been told you, Elijah said that he
and the priests of Baal should lay a bullock on the
altar, and that the God who should send fire from
heaven to consume it, should be owned as the true
God. And all the people said, " The word is
good." And as they were for it, the priests did
not dare object. So they prepared their altar,
and laid the pieces of the bullock on the wood,
" and they called on the name of Baal from morning even until noon, saying, O Baal, answer us:
but there was no voice, nor any that heard ;" and
they at length became quite wild, and leaped up
and down in their rage upon the altar.

When at noon they had quite tired themselves,

and no spark of fire was to be seen, Elijah began to mock them; and he said, " Cry aloud, for he is a god; either he is talking, or he is pursuing, or he is on a journey; or, perhaps, he sleeps, and must be awaked." A pretty god, truly, who would not regard so many of his priests, with the king and queen, and their subjects,—and would not give them even the tiny boon of a little fire in this their utmost need!

However, they thought they would have another try for it; and so they cried louder and louder, and they cut themselves with knives and lancets till they were covered with blood; vainly thinking, that Baal would pity them in their wretched state. But it was all of no use; for though they went on in this way " till the time of the offering of the evening sacrifice," yet there was neither " voice, nor any to answer, nor any that regarded."

What, then, was their god " talking," and could not pay attention to several things at once? No, for he could not speak. Was he pursuing after some foe? No, he had no power to seize on the feeblest of his enemies.   Was he, then, on a journey?   No, for he was unable to move a limb, or take a step.   Was he, then, asleep?   No, he was never awake; he was only a block of wood, or a piece of stone, or a plaster figure,—a mere form, a vanity, a nothing!   Of course, then, he could not give them one spark of fire..

The multitude of the people had all been around Baal's priests, to see what they could do, through the day, till they were quite weary, and they had no hope of any fire from Baal; and now Elijah said to them. " Come near to me ;" and they came. And he prepared an altar according to his wishes, making a deep and wide trench all around it.

And the wood was laid upon the altar, and the bullock upon the wood.   And Elijah bade the people pour on the sacrifice, and on the wood, twelve barrels of water, which ran about the altar, and filled the trench ; so that it was very plain that not a spark of fire was hid in the altar, or in anything upon it.

We may not be so foolish as the people who

worshipped Baal; we may not bow down to a
stock or a stone: but if we love any object more
than we love God, that is our idol it; fills the
place of God in our hearts, and God will not be
pleased with us, or hold us guiltless.'   It was not
without reason that the Apostle John said to his
friends, " Little children, keep yourselves from
idols."*   Each one should pray for grace, that he
may say from his heart,*

> " The dearest idol I have known,
>   Whate'er that idol be ;
>   Help me to tear it from thy throne,
>   And worship only thee !"

QUESTIONS.

1. How may we know whether persons reverence God or not ?

2. What does sin do ?

3. What are those who are not quite on the Saviour's side ?

4. What should every one say ?

5. Should we follow the greatest number in matters of religion ?

6. May we follow the great, and rich, if they do not serve God.

7. Is the object which we most love our idol ?

8. What did St. John say to professing Christians ?

9. What should each pray for grace that he may say ?

STORY XX.

THE PRAYER OF ELIJAH.

AND now Elijah drew near to the altar, and with his heart nearer to the throne of grace. And the eyes of Ahab, of the priests of Baal, and of the vast multitude, were fixed on him. Most likely they made a large circle around him; and he lifted up his eyes, and stretched forth his hands to the heavens, and said, " Lord God of Abraham, Isaac, and of Jacob, let it be known this day that thou art God in Israel, and that I have done all these things at thy word. Hear me, O Lord, hear me; that this people may know that thou art the Lord God, when thou hast turned their hearts back again."[1]

This was a very simple, and a very beautiful

THE PRAYER OF ELIJAH.

prayer. It was not full of vain repetitions, like that of the priests of Baal, who cried, " O Baal, hear us," from the morning till the evening. The prayer was very brief: God does not hear us for our long or fine speaking. The poor woman of Canaan who came to our Lord, said, " Lord, help me !" The publican cried out, " God, be merciful to me, a sinner !" And the thief on the cross only begged that he would " remember " him. And these were all excellent prayers.'

Elijah called upon the Lord, as " the God of Abraham, Isaac, and Jacob ;" and he is the God of every one, who, as they did, put their trust in him, and call upon him in every age. And will he be my God if I do so ? He will.

Observe what pleas the prophet used with God; he asked him to answer his prayer for his own glory, that it " might be known that he," and not Baal, was " God in Israel;" and that all might be sure that he was the servant of the Lord. And God heard him.

When he had just ended his prayer, the heavens

were opened, and " the fire of the Lord fell, and
consumed the burnt-sacrifice, and the wood, and
the stones, and the dust, and licked up the water
that was in the trench." [3]

No doubt but that this large company was
terror-struck, when they saw the mass of flame
fall on the altar: " and they fell on their faces,
and they said, The Lord, he is the God!" [4]   They
repeated it, to show how fully their minds were
convinced of this great truth.   They would have
been as hard, and as stupid as the rocks of the
mountain on which they stood, if they had not
done so. [5]

Yes, " the Lord he is God;" the only living and
true God.   There is none so great, wise, holy,
powerful, just, faithful, nor so gracious as he is.
He alone can give rain, and fruitful seasons; he
alone can pardon and justify, can sanctify and save
any one of our lost race.

And when the great stream of fire came down
from the skies, did it convert Ahab, and all the
priests, and the people ?   No, we are certain that

it did not; though one should have thought, that such a solemn sight would have brought them all to God in earnest prayer. Men are often alarmed by God's judgments, without being humbled or changed. God spake many times in terror to Pharaoh, but his heart was not softened: he was Pharaoh still. So, many who have had great afflictions, and solemn warnings, are spared, but not converted, or brought to God through Jesus Christ.⁶ How very sad will be their last account, should they live and die in their sins!

And now, how glad would the priests of Baal have been to have escaped: but they could not; for Elijah said to the people, " Seize the prophets of Baal, let not one of them escape ; and they took them, and brought them down to the brook Kishon, and slew them there." ⁷ For God had commanded, that if a son, or daughter, or wife, or friend, should entice any one to worship idols, they should be cut off from the land,⁸ Deut. xiii. 6—11. So, at last, shall all the enemies of the Lord perish.

There are multitudes of our race who every day

bow the knee to gods such as Baal; to senseless
stocks and stones, the work of men's hands; which
" have eyes, but see not; ears, but hear not;
hands, but handle not; and feet, but walk not;
nor can they speak, or do any thing to help their
silly worshippers.' How we should pity and pray
for them; nor should we rest satisfied with pity
and prayer; we should try and send good men,
with the blessed Bible, to teach them about Jesus
Christ, and heaven, and the way to it, and all that
they ought to believe and do.[10] For " how can
they hear without a preacher, and how can they
preach, except they be sent?"

If the people in London were all dying for want
of bread, and they who lived in the country had a
great abundance, and they would not send them
any to save them from starving, what should we
say of them. And would God be pleased with
them?

QUESTIONS.

1. Can you repeat the prayer of Elijah?

2. What were the prayers of the woman of Canaan, of the publican, and of the dying thief?

3. How did God answer the prayer of Elijah?

4. What did the people do and say, when they saw the fire fall from the skies?

5. What would they have been if they had not done so?

6. Do afflictions and judgments always convert people?

7. What did Elijah bid the people do to the wicked prophets of Baal?

8. What was God's command about idolaters?

9. What gods do multitudes of our race still worship?

10. What should we do for these people?

M

STORY XXI.

THE LITTLE CLOUD.

It seems likely that a tent had been pitched for Ahab on the side of Mount Carmel; and now, when the great business of the day was ended, Elijah bade him go and eat and drink, for God would surely visit the land in mercy: "There is," said he, "a sound of abundance of rain." When the clouds which threaten God's judgments, are scattered, our souls should be filled with thankfulness and holy joy. How happy, and how safe, was Noah in the ark, though the storms were falling on a lost world: [1]

> "So may I sing, in Jesus safe,
>   Tho' storms of wrath around me fall;
> Conscious how high my hopes are rais'd,
>   Beyond what shakes this earthly ball."

A good man has eyes, even the eyes of faith, which many around him have not. Thus Moses saw " Him who is invisible," and he feared not the wrath of Pharaoh. What an ear is the ear of faith. Elijah, with his ear, heard what no one else heard, " the sound of abundance of rain." So, God has said, " the people shall praise him,—yea, all the people shall praise him ;"—and the eye of faith already sees the nations turning to the Lord, and, even now, hears the glad hosannas rising to heaven from a redeemed world.

And the prophet went up to the summit of the mountain, from whence he could see the vast ocean ; and " he fell down upon the earth, and put his face between his knees ;" showing his great reverence of the divine Majesty.' Though we are not told what he said, there can be no doubt he thanked God that he had heard his prayer, and sent fire to consume the sacrifice. And, most likely, he prayed that God would complete his work of mercy, and send rain,—and turn the hearts of the people from the worship of dumb idols.

For though God has promised to protect, guide, supply, comfort, pardon, and save his servants, yet he has declared, that he will confer all these blessings in answer to their prayers.

No doubt, Elijah, when " on the ground, with his face between his knees," was asking God to fulfil his promise without delay ; and he expected, though as yet there were no clouds, or the least sign of rain, that God would very soon give some token that his prayer was heard. So he called his servant, and he sent him to the point from whence he could see the most of the great deep, to examine whether he could discern any cloud ; but he went and came back, and did not see any thing more than the burning heavens, which they had so long seen. But Elijah said, " Go again, seven times." God had said, he would give rain, and he knew that his word could not fail.

And the servant went up again and again, and saw nothing ; but the seventh time he perceived a small change ; and on his return, he said, " Behold, there ariseth a little cloud out of the sea, like a man's hand. And Elijah said, Go, say unto Ahab, Prepare thy chariot, and get thee down, that the rain stop thee not."

And the heavens were soon black with clouds, and the wind arose, " and there was a great rain." God can not only bless his servants, but he can do it abundantly; he can, and he will do for them even far beyond all that they can " ask or think."³

" And the hand of the Lord was on Elijah," giving him more than his natural strength, and to do honour to the king, he ran, as a herald, before his chariot, to the very entrance of Jezreel, the town in which he lived. If Ahab had felt as he ought, he would have invited him into his chariot to sit with him.

From this account of the prophet and " the little cloud," that brought so much rain, we may learn many things.

We may learn, that it is God who gives us rain and sunshine, and all the blessings which we enjoy; and we should see him in the sunshine and the rain, and praise him for them, and for our daily and hourly comforts.[4]

And as the prophet did not give up praying for rain till the " little cloud " appeared ; so, we should never give up asking for the great things which God has promised to bestow, till we receive them from the Divine hands.[5]

As Elijah looked and prayed for the showers of rain, so we should look and pray for the gracious influence of the Holy Spirit. These come down as the rain and the dew.[6] The rain does not fall according to the merit of the creature, but on " the evil and the good, on the thankful and on the unthankful." So does divine influence,—or it would never have fallen on the poor thief, or on Manasseh.[6] How gently does the rain often fall on the earth! It is thus with respect to Divine grace. So the Lord gently opened the heart of Lydia, to attend to the things spoken by Paul.[6] And who can prevent the rain from falling whenever God is pleased to send it? So it is God sends the blessings of his grace. If God bids them fall on us, no one can hinder them.⁶ And if we ask him, he will be sure to confer them on us.

From " the little cloud," we may learn, that we should not despise the day of small things. We should not do so in ourselves, or in others.⁷ If we have any good desires, any secret wishes to serve the Lord, let us bless God for them; let us ask him for more grace, and we shall find a day of " small things " advance to a day of greater things. Nicodemus, who " at first came to Jesus by night," at last confessed him before all the great men of his nation.⁸

Nor should we despise the day of " small things," as it respects others; if a dear child, or youth, loves to retire to read the Bible, or to hear, or to speak of the things of God, it is matter of thanksgiving.⁹

There are now millions of children in infant and sabbath schools who are taught to read the Scriptures, and who are training " up in the nurture and admonition of the Lord." This great work was very small in its beginning,—it was but a " little cloud, not bigger than a man's hand."

A few years ago the Book of God was scarce, and some good men met to plan a way for its increase; and now they have sent many millions of copies through the world; and they are multiplying them every day,—though at first the work was but " a little cloud, not bigger than a man's hand." [10]

So some of the servants of the Lord, when the heathen lands were lying " in darkness and the shadow of death," thought that they would send a few messengers to them with " the glad tidings " of the Gospel; and they are now become a great multitude, and they are gone to men of " every tongue, and people, and kindred, and nation." At first nothing was seen but " a little cloud, not bigger than a man's hand." [10]

And the work must increase, till " the kingdoms of the world are become the kingdoms of our God, and of his Christ; and he shall reign for ever and ever."

QUESTIONS.

1. What may the good man say who has fled for refuge to Christ, as Noah did to the ark?

2. How did Elijah show his great reverence of God?

3. What can God do, and what will he do, for his servants who call upon him?

4. What does God give us, and what should we do?

5. What should we never give up?

6. In what respects does the rain fall like divine influence?

7. In what respects should we not despise the day of " small things?"

8. How did a day of small things become one of greater things in Nicodemus?

9. What is matter of thanksgiving?

10. What efforts are making which were in their origin but as the little cloud?

STORY XXII.

—❋—

THE FLIGHT OF ELIJAH.

WHEN Ahab had got home, he made haste to tell Jezebel all he had seen and heard. How Baal's prophets had called on their god, and bawled as loud as they could, and that he could not hear them, or send them a spark of fire; but that Elijah only began praying, when, lo, the heavens opened, and a mass of flames fell on his sacrifice, and consumed it, and the stones of the altar, and dried up the twelve barrels of water he had poured in the trench. And how all the people had fallen on their faces, and owned Elijah's God as the true God; and finally, how the four hundred and fifty prophets of Baal had been slain.[1]

He told her, that Elijah had done all this;

THE FLIGHT OF ELIJAH.

whereas he should have said, it was the Lord, in answer to the prayers of Elijah. It looks as if he thought that the prophet had wrought this miracle by some secret craft of his own, by which he had deceived the people ; and so, if this were the case, Baal might yet be a god. How true is the saying of the wise man,—" Bray a fool in a mortar, yet will his foolishness not depart from him."²

Now the torrents of rain were falling over all the land, how ought he and his subjects to have adored and praised the living and the true God, the giver not only of the rain, but of " every good and perfect gift."³

But Jezebel, when she heard of the death of Baal's prophets, was in a great rage, and she sent a messenger to Elijah, saying, " So let the gods do to me, and more also, if I make not thy life, as the life of one of them, by to-morrow about this time !"

She would have been more likely to have cut him off, if she had not sent to give him warning. See how God takes " the wise in their own craftiness." But she made sure, now she knew where he was, of slaying him. Just as Pharaoh did of destroying Israel. He said, " I will arise," I will do what I please, and so on. And he did so; but he and his hosts perished in the mighty waters.⁴

It is a proud word for any mortal to say, that he WILL do this or that " to-morrow."⁵ But Jezebel said, she would cut off the prophet to-morrow. How did she know she might not be dead before the dawn of to-morrow? Herod said, that he would kill Peter to-morrow; but the night before, God sent his angel to open the prison-doors, and so he was saved from his cruel hands.⁶ The power of life and death is not in the keeping of any one of our race.

And Elijah was much afraid; and he arose and fled in haste to Beersheba, which was not in the kingdom of Ahab. There, as he wished to be alone, to think of the sad state of things, and to pray that God would appear for his cause in the land of Israel, he left his servant. But he ought not to have fled; for God, who had preserved him so remarkably, would still have kept him from evil, and he might have done much to bring back the people to the worship of God. The words of another prophet might have been addressed to him, —" Who art thou, that thou art afraid of a man that shall die, and of the son of man, whose breath is in his nostrils, and forgettest the Lord thy Maker, and the former of the heavens?"' The hands of the strongest of the Lord's servants have now and then " hung down," and the hearts of those who have had most courage, have sometimes been ready to faint.

After he had left his servant at Beersheba, he arose, and went a day's journey into the wilderness, and sat down, hungry, thirsty, and weary, under a juniper-tree. Here he earnestly begged of the Lord, that his days might close. Most likely he expected that Baal would have been quite cast away, and the worship of the true God restored in its purity. But it was not so; and he was grieved at heart to see the wickedness of the people. So he lay down to sleep beneath a juniper-tree. And an angel awoke him with a touch, and said, " Arise, and eat. And, behold, there was a cake baken on the coals, and a cruse of water at his head; and he did eat and drink, and lay down again." And the angel awoke him a second time, and would have him take more food; and he did so; " and he went in the strength of that meat forty days and forty nights, till he came to Horeb, the mount of God."

God sent his angel that the prophet might know, that even in that wilderness he was not without a Divine protector. A child of God, wherever he may be, is always in the dominion of his Father. " His place of defence, wherever he may dwell, " is the munitions of rocks, his bread shall be given him, and his water shall be sure." And God can support the human frame with food or without it.*

In all our straights, if we " seek first the kingdom of God, and his righteousness," the Lord has assured us, that " all other things shall be added to us."°

And in all the dangers to which we are exposed, if we fly to the shadow of the Almighty wings, no weapon that is formed against us shall prosper, and every tongue rising against us in judgment, the Lord will condemn it."

QUESTIONS.

1. What did Ahab tell Jezebel?
2. What does the wise man say of the obstinate sinner?
3. What ought Ahab and his subjects to have done?
4. What did Pharaoh say,—and what became of him and his hosts?
5. What is a proud word for any mortal to say?
6. What did Herod say,—and how did God save Peter?
7. What does God say to his fearful servant?
8. Mention some of the privileges of God's children?
9. What should we do in all our straights?
10. How may we be safe in all dangers?

STORY XXIII.

THE LORD'S INTERVIEW WITH ELIJAH.

At last, in his wanderings in the desert, Elijah came to Mount Horeb, on which Moses had seen the bush in flames, but not consumed, and from the midst of which God spake to him. Here the prophet found a cave; and, for a season, he took up his abode in it. God knew where he was; and wherever his servants are, or in whatever condition, his eyes are upon them, and that for their good. He was with Joseph in the dungeon; with David, when hunted by Saul as a partridge on the mountains; with John in the Isle of Patmos; and with Paul, when driven about on the mighty waters.[1]

And as Elijah was sitting in this cave, he heard

a voice,—it was the voice of the Lord,—and it said, "What doest thou here, Elijah?" Is this the place, where there are none to hear thy word, in which thou canst glorify me, or do any good to Israel? Why didst thou flee? Was not my almighty arm sufficient for thy protection? What doest thou here? If we get out of the path of our duty, God will send or come after us.' You know how he sent a tempest after Jonah.

Should the Lord come and say to him who is often in wicked company, or at home on the sabbath, when he ought to be in the house of God, or living in any sin, " What doest thou here?" what answer could he give? Certainly, none that could please the Lord.' And every one shall be obliged to give an account of himself unto God.

And Elijah answered,—" I have been very jealous for the Lord God of Hosts; for the children of Israel have forsaken thy covenant, thrown down thy altar, and slain thy prophets with the sword; and I, even I only, am left, and they seek to take away my life."

N

This was as good an answer as he could make; and it was true that he had been very zealous for God's glory, and for the welfare of Israel,—and yet they had scorned him and his advice, and had contemned God. It is a great trouble to a faithful servant of the Lord, " to spend his strength for nought, and in vain;" but yet he should not be hasty in leaving the post in which God has placed him. In due time he may reap if he does not faint. If the harvest be not good this year, we must not give up sowing, for it may be abundant in the next.

Elijah was mistaken in supposing that he was left alone in Israel to serve God. He had forgotten that good Obadiah had hid one hundred of the faithful servants of the Lord in two caves, and had fed them with the best provision he could procure. And now God told him, there were many thousands who had not bowed the knee to Baal, and who had not kissed or worshipped his image. And, no doubt, in the worst times, there are more good people than we are apt to imagine.[*]

And now the voice said, "Go forth, and stand upon the mount before the Lord." God was about to give him a wonderful display of his presence, power, and glory, to show him how able he was to protect his servants in times of the greatest danger. "And the Lord passed by,"—and, to awaken the attention of the prophet, and fill him with holy reverence of the Divine Majesty, "a great and strong wind rent the mountains, and brake in pieces the rocks," to show him how able he was to break the hard hearts of his hearers. And after the tempest there was an earthquake, and after the earthquake a fire; but the Lord did not speak to the prophet from the midst of the storm, the earthquake, or the fire.

But after the fire, the prophet heard "a still small voice;" and he went and stood at the entrance of the cave, and it said, "What doest thou here, Elijah?" And he felt that God was present,— "and he wrapped his face in his mantle,"—from holy reverence, as the angels veil their faces with their wings,—or from holy shame, that he should

N 2

have been so fearful as to flee from his duty when God was so near, and so able and willing to shield him from evil. And God sent him on various errands in his service.

No doubt the Lord gave him at this time reason to believe that his request, that he might enter into glory, would soon be granted, as he charged him to appoint Elisha in his room. In every age God will, by his Holy Spirit, raise up and qualify men to know and to do his will.[5]

God sometimes speaks to the sinner amidst the earthquake, and the tempest, as he did to the jailor at Philippi; but, more frequently, by the still voice of conscience, of his word, and of his Spirit. God often speaks to the sinner when no one knows it but himself, and in a "still small voice."[6]

The earthquake, the tempest, and fire, remind us of Sinai, and of the law; but the "still small voice" of God speaking to poor sinners by the Lord Jesus. How thankful should we be, that we are not come to the terrors of Sinai, but "unto Mount Sion, and unto the city of the living God, the heavenly Jerusalem, and to an innumerable company of angels; to the general assembly, and church of the first-born, which are written in heaven, and to Jesus the Mediator of the New Covenant, and to the blood of sprinkling, which speaketh better things than that of Abel." '

QUESTIONS.

1. Mention some cases in which God was with his servant in trouble?

2. What will God do if we get out of the path of duty?

3. Should the Lord say to the sinner, Where art thou? what answer could he give?

4. What are there in the worst times?

5. What will God do in every age?

6. How does God often speak to the sinner?

7. Whither are real Christians come?

STORY XXIV.

—✳—

THE CALL OF ELIJAH.

AND Elijah left the cave on Mount Horeb, and journeyed to attend to several things which the Lord charged him to do. One of these was to appoint Elisha to be a prophet in his room.

Now Elisha was a farmer, and he had very much land; for when Elijah found him in the fields, his servants were guiding eleven ploughs, and he himself was holding the twelfth; for Elisha knew, what we have often heard, that

> " He who by the plough would thrive,
> Himself must either hold or drive." [1]

Some of the most eminent of God's servants in every age, who have been " diligent in business, have been fervent in spirit, serving the Lord."

THE CALL OF ELISHA.

Moses was a shepherd, and looked after the flocks of Jethro, his father-in-law, on Mount Horeb. When the angel came to Gideon, he found him threshing wheat. David was taken from the sheep-fold. Amos was a herdsman, and a gatherer of wild figs. And the prophet Zechariah says of himself, " I am a husbandman, taught to keep cattle from my youth." And so it has been in every age. Not long since, when God designed to reveal his holy word to the people of the East in their own tongues, he called a poor artizan from a little cottage in Leicestershire; and, taught of God, he has done the great work.*²

And so Elijah found Elisha ploughing; and he passed by him, and threw his mantle over his shoulders. No doubt this good man was one of the Lord's hidden ones; and, whilst the court and the great people were gone after Baal, he and his household served the Lord.

Elijah does not seem to have said any thing to

---

* Professor Carey.

Elisha; but, no doubt, the Holy Spirit told him why he threw his mantle on him, and that he was to leave his work, and his farm, and to follow Elijah, and serve the Lord as his prophet.

So he left his oxen, and ran to overtake Elijah, who seemed as if he would go away without holding any converse with him. He soon came up with him, and said, that he would forsake all, and do as the Lord had bade him. But he asked his leave first to go and kiss his father and mother, and bid them farewell; and the prophet gave him leave.

God's people, according to his promise, are " a willing people in the day of his power;" willing, when he renews them by his Spirit, to come out from the world, and to be his. " Other lords," they say, " have had dominion over us, but henceforward by thy name will we be called." [1]

And Elijah stayed till he came back from his father's house. Elisha then slew a yoke of oxen, and the meat was dressed with the wood of which the plough and other things used by him in the field were made, to show that he quite gave up his former labours to engage in the service of God. Then he made a great feast for all the people; and, no doubt, as he bade them farewell, he warned them not to worship Baal, but " to cleave to the Lord with full purpose of heart," in the strength of his grace to be his servants for ever. And now he arose, and followed Elijah, " and ministered to him."

Had he consulted his wordly interest, or taken the counsel of his carnal friends, he would never have left his farm, or so much as thought of following Elijah. For there was no hope of a good living for him, or of the honours, or riches, or pleasures of the world. He had nothing to expect in this world but contempt, suffering, and death, perhaps, from Ahab or Jezebel. But he was a good servant of the Lord; his heart was right with him, and he sought his glory far before all other things.⁴

Nor can such by any means lose their reward. " Despised and rejected of men," like their Master, they shall be owned by him as his in the great assembly at the last day. " Verily I say unto you," said the Lord Jesus, " every one that hath forsaken houses, or brethren, or sisters, or father, or mother, or wife, or children, or lands, for my sake, shall receive a hundred fold, and shall inherit everlasting life."

How soon Elisha did as Elijah wished him! He made haste, as every one ought to do, to obey God's commandments.' It is always thus when any one hears the voice of the Lord. Thus, when our Lord saw Peter, and Andrew his brother, casting a net into the sea, he saith unto them, " Follow me!" and a Divine power was given with the word, and they instantly left their nets, and followed him.

And every one of the Lord's servants hears the voice of the Holy Spirit, that " still small voice," which makes him a different person, even " a new creature." But how may I know whether I have heard the voice of the Saviour calling me ?

Why, all who have heard his voice, see things in

a new light; "old things are passed away, lo, all things are become new." Do I do so?

All who have heard his voice, seek by humble and fervent prayer for the favour of God,—they desire to gain it more than any thing else besides. And do I?

They are sorry from their heart, that they have offended the good and gracious God in thought, word, and deed. And is this the case with me? They are made sincerely willing to part with any sin, however dear it may be to them. And am I?

They rely simply and entirely on the merits of the Lord Jesus for access to God, for acceptance with him, for pardon, righteousness, and eternal life. And do I?

They love the Saviour, and they take him for their prophet, priest, and king. Do I do so?

They are constantly trying, in the strength of God's grace, to imitate his holy example.* Is this my case?

If this be the case, why then I have heard the voice of the Saviour, I am one of his servants;

and, when I have done and suffered his will here below, I shall know for myself what he meant when he said, " Where I am, there also shall my servant be !"   Blessed knowledge !'

QUESTIONS.

1. What did Elijah know ?

2. Whom did God call to translate his holy word into some of the tongues of the east ?

3. What do the Lord's people say to him ?

4. What was Elisha ?

5. What did Elisha do ?

6. Mention the seven marks of the characters of those who have heard Christ's voice ?

7. What shall I know at last if I am one who has heard the Saviour's voice.

THE WIDOW'S POT OF OIL.

STORY XXV.

THE WIDOW'S POT OF OIL.

THERE was a poor widow who lived in the days of Elisha, whose history is wonderful. She was the wife of one of the sons of the prophets; he was a very good man, for he not only feared to offend God, but he was always trying, by the help of Divine grace, to do everything to please him.[1] No doubt he was one of the many thousands who would not "bow the knee to Baal."

But at last he died; it is not known how, whether suddenly, or after a long illness; nor does it matter how, or where, or when a good man dies; for his end is sure to be peace, and he is sure to enter into glory.[2]

It is likely he had but very little, if any thing,

for preaching. God's faithful servants are not so much concerned to enrich themselves with the fleece, as to save the flock; so he died very poor, —and, what was much worse, he died greatly in debt. We are sure his debts were not incurred "in riotous living," or in any improper way, because "he feared the Lord;" perhaps what he owed was for bread, which they were obliged to have in the time of the famine. We ought to wear coarser garments, and be content with meaner fare, and to work very hard, or to do any thing we can, rather than get into debt.[*]

And it is likely this good man did so. But, then, how came he to be so greatly in debt? Perhaps Baal's prophets took much of what he had for the support of their idol worship; perhaps he had met with great losses; perhaps he had helped the poor persecuted people of God in that time of sorrow beyond his ability; or, perhaps, he had been very long ill, and had been obliged to spend his substance.

When he died, the poor widow knew not what

to do. She sold one article of furniture after another, till she had scarcely any thing left. It is true, she had two sons who were very dear to her; and, no doubt, she hoped that in time they would labour, and help her, so that she might be able to pay her debts. But what made her case now very trying was, that her creditors would not wait any longer; but they said, that if she did not pay them in a little while, they would seize the two dear boys, and sell them into bondage for six years.

So the poor widow was in the depth of trouble; and she thought she would go and lay her whole case before Elisha. We should help the widow and fatherless, and the distressed, by our counsels and our prayers; and, as far as we can, with our substance. " He that hath this world's goods, and seeth his brother have need, and shutteth up the bowels of his compassiou from him, how dwelleth the love of God in him?"

Now Elisha, no doubt, had been told by God what he should say to her. So he asked her,

What she had in the house?"   And she said, Thy
hand-maid hath not any thing in the house save
a pot of oil."   And he told her she must become
an oil merchant; and though her stock was a very
small one to begin with, he would tell her how
it would be increased.   It is a charity to give the
poor bread enough for a day; but it is a much
greater good to put them in a way to earn their
living.'

  Then the prophet said, " Go, borrow thee
vessels abroad of all thy neighbours, even empty
vessels, borrow not a few.   And when thou art
come in, thou shalt shut the door upon thee, and
upon thy sons, and shalt pour out into all those
vessels, and thou shalt set aside those that are full."

  She did not say, as some would, Of what use
will it be to borrow empty vessels!   How can one
pot of oil become many!   Who ever heard of
such a strange project!   The people who hear of
it will laugh me to scorn!   I thought he would
have given me some money; or that he would
have said, he would.try and raise a subscription

for me among his friends; or have found out some plan by which I might earn my daily bread, my creditors be satisfied, and my dear boys saved from being sold into bondage. But to think of borrowing empty barrels, tubs, and pans, surely this seems only mocking me in my distress!'

No, she did not say any thing like this. The servants of the Lord are blessed with faith in his power, goodness, and love. And this was the case with the poor widow. So she went and borrowed empty vessels of all sorts, till she had her house full of them. And then, as the prophet had told her, she shut her door, that she might not be disturbed, and the better see, admire, adore, and praise the great Giver of all good.

And now her dear boys brought one vessel after another to her, and she poured oil out of her pot into them, till they were all full; so that they had not one left to receive any more. How would she, and her children, be ready to leap for joy!'

So she ran to tell Elisha what had taken place,

o

and how the Lord had helped and delivered her in the time of her deep distress.   He will never forsake those who put their trust "under the shadow of his wings."

Then Elisha bade her go and sell the oil, and pay her debts, and reserve the rest for the support of her family.

The oil brought a large sum of money; no doubt, like the wine which our Lord gave by miracle at Cana, it was better than any other that could be bought.   Thus it was her dear boys were saved from being sold into bondage.   God is the God of the widow and the fatherless, and he will provide for them.   We should help and plead for them.   God is angry with those who do them any wrong.

God is as able to help and provide for us in the ways of his providence, as he then was to aid the poor widow by miracle.   His bounty has followed us in a perpetual stream; and will it not still flow on by our side, and shall we not drink of it for ever?

When in straights and difficulties, let us think of the widow's pot of oil, and cast our care on him who has given us so many proofs that he careth for us.[9]

Let us think of the instructions of the great Teacher; " Take no thought," said he, " for your life ; what ye shall eat, or what ye shall drink; nor yet for your body, what ye shall put on. Is not the life more than meat, and the body than raiment? Behold the fowls of the air; for they sow not, neither do they reap, nor gather into barns; yet your heavenly Father feedeth them. Are ye not much better than they? Seek first the kingdom of God, and his righteousness, and all these things shall be added unto you."[10]

QUESTIONS.

1. What was the character of the husband of the poor widow ?

2. What is of no moment in reference to the good man ?

3. What ought we to do rather than get into debt ?

4. How should we help the widow, and fatherless, and those who are in trouble ?

5. What is a great charity ?

6. What did the widow not say ?

7. What was done with the empty vessels ?

8. How has God's bounty, and how will it, follow us ?

9. Of what should we think in straights and difficulties ?

10. What did the great Teacher say in reference to food and raiment ?

STORY XXVI.

THE SHUNEMITE'S SON.

As the people of God were in much trouble on account of wicked Ahab, and the priests of Baal, Elisha used to journey from place to place to encourage and comfort them. Among the towns he passed through, one was called Shunem. Here a generous and a pious woman lived, who knew that he was "a holy man of God," and she constrained him by her kindness to come into her house to repose and refresh himself.

Moreover, she said to her husband, "Let us make a little chamber, I pray thee, on the wall," to which he may have easy access, and where he may enjoy meditation, being removed from the noise and bustle of the family, and "let us set there for him a bed, and a table, and a stool, and a candlestick; and it shall be when he cometh, that he shall turn in thither."[1] And they built the chamber and furnished it.

Elisha, and his servant, came into it, and the mistress of the house very kindly provided for them. So the prophet, to show how much he felt obliged, asked her, if he could do any thing for her? But she said he could not. " I dwell," said she, " among my own people and kindred, and am contented and happy."

But as his servant had observed that she had no child, the prophet asked God to give her a son,— and God heard his prayer. Dutiful and pious children are an especial, and a gracious gift of God.[2]

And, no doubt, the parents were much pleased with their little boy; and he delighted to go about with his father. One morning as he went with him into his fields to look at the reapers, he was suddenly taken very ill; perhaps he was struck with the heat of the sun, as he cried, " My head! My head!" And his father bade a lad take him up, and carry him home to his mother. And he did so; and his mother nursed him on her knees till noon, and then he died. There is often, though we may not know it, but " a step between us and death."³ How ought we to be ready for our great change!

And now, what could she do more than resign him to God who had given him. She had, however, a secret hope, that he would be restored to life, through the prayers of Elisha. So she laid the dead child on the bed of the prophet, and sent to her husband to ask that one of the servants might take her to Mount Carmel.

Now she was used to go to worship there on the sabbath, and at other seasons of special devotion, but her husband could not think why she wished to go now; but yet he granted her request.

And as Elisha was walking out on the mountain, he saw her afar off, and he said to Gehazi, " Behold, yonder is that Shunemite. Run now, I pray thee, to meet her, and say unto her, " Is it well with thee? Is it well with thy husband? Is it well with the child? And she answered; It is well!"⁴

When she came to the prophet she was full of trouble, and seized him by his feet, and told him all the sad tale of her sorrow; nor would she loose him, till she had some reason to hope that he would try and help her.

Perhaps he had some other purpose in his mind, and wished to be excused from going to Shunem; for he sent Gehazi, and bade him make the utmost haste, and lay his master's staff on the child, expecting, in answer to his earnest prayer, that the child might be raised to life again.

But the mother told him most solemnly that he might send Gehazi, if he pleased, but that she would not go back unless he would go with her.

And as they were going, the servant met them; and he said, that he had done as his master had told him, and had spoken to the child, but that the child neither spoke nor heard. Perhaps, as Elijah was obliged to go, he had not prayed that the Lord would own the laying on of the staff for bringing him back to life.

And Elisha went into his little chamber on the

wall, and there he found the dead child laid on his bed. And he shut the door, and prayed earnestly to the Lord that the child might be restored to life. Then he walked about hither and thither in the habitation, and prayed. So the Lord heard, and answered, for " the child sneezed seven times, and opened his eyes." Now he bade his servant call the mother; and when she saw her son alive, to honour the prophet, " she fell at his feet, and bowed herself to the ground." Who can tell how gladly she clasped her little boy in her arms, and went out of the chamber.

But how could she say that it was well with the child, when it was dead? Why, because she believed the delightful truth, that " the Lord reigneth;" so that her darling boy did not die without his permission. She knew that affliction and health, prosperity and adversity, life and death, take their orders from him. " Son of man," said he to Ezekiel, " I take away the delight of thine eyes with a stroke!"

She knew that all which God does is right and

good; and therefore well.[6] He is infinite in wisdom, and it cannot be otherwise. When we imagine it is not the case, it is because we see only a part of the Divine purposes.[7] Jacob thought at one time that every thing was against him; but when he heard that Joseph was lord over all the land of Egypt, and when he saw the wagons which he had sent to bring him and all his family into that land, he said, "It is enough!"[8] It is well!

And, no doubt, she knew, that if the dear boy should not return again to life, it would be well with him, for that his spirit would be happy for ever.[8]

But she believed, that, in answer to the prayers of the prophet, she should clasp her dear child alive again to her fond bosom, and so she said, "It is well!"[9]

And when a dear child, or brother, or sister, or parent, or friend, is taken away by death to the kingdom of glory, the departure will be well, even for ourselves, if we are moved by it to "number our days, and to apply our hearts to real wisdom."[10] If we are led by the solemn stroke, to consider our state, and to " fly for refuge to Christ, as the hope set before us in the Gospel:" [10] if we are induced earnestly to pray for grace, that we may so pass through the things that are seen and are temporal, as to reach and enjoy the things that are not seen and are eternal.[10]

~~~~~~~~~~~~~~~~~~

QUESTIONS.

1. What did the woman of Shunem propose to do for Elisha?

2. What are dutiful and pious children?

3. What is there often, though we may not know it?

4. What did Gehazi say to the mother of the little boy, and what was her reply?

5. Mention a reason why the mother said, " It is well," though her child was dead?

6. Mention another.

7. Why is it that we even imagine that God's plans are not good and right?

8. What did Jacob say at different times?

9. Mention two other reasons why the mother said, " It is well!"

10. How will it appear that the departure of a pious friend is " well" in reference to ourselves?

STORY XXVII.

THE VISION OF ISAIAH.

I⊤ appears from the Bible, that in old times God was often pleased to reveal his will to his servants in a vision; or, by a strong impression of things on their minds, that they might properly know and discharge their duty.

Isaiah was favoured with a sublime vision. He beheld, in solemn thought, the Lord Jesus, seated on a throne, " high and lifted up," * in all his majesty and glory; and " the skirts of his flowing robes filled the temple." As there is no monarch like to the divine Saviour, so there is no throne like his. His throne is " lifted up " above all other thrones.

---

* John xii. 41.

Before him stood the seraphim; these are happy spirits who were filled with love and zeal for the divine Majesty. Each of them had six wings; with two they veiled their faces, as if dazzled with the awful glories of their Lord; with two they covered their feet, as unworthy to stand in his holy presence; and with two they did fly, showing the joyful readiness with which they obey the commands of their Sovereign.

These happy spirits cried aloud to each other, and they said, "Holy, holy, holy, is the Lord of hosts, the whole earth is full of his glory!"[2] That is, the Divine excellence is above our thoughts,—there is no bounds to it. All beings, and all worlds, are subject to his control: the whole earth is full of the glory of his works of creation, providence, and grace.[3] And "the posts of the doors" of the vast temple which the prophet saw, and the temple itself, seemed to shake and tremble at this display of the divine Majesty.

When the prophet saw this glorious vision, his mind was deeply affected with the unlikeness between himself and God. "Woe is me," he said, "for I am undone; because I am a man of unclean lips, and I dwell in the midst of a people of unclean lips: for mine eyes have seen the king, the Lord of hosts!" Those who have right views of God, are always abased before him.

The mind of the prophet was so much affected with a sense of his guilt, that he thought he could never again speak for God, or go with his messages. He was struck dumb, and confounded before his Lord and Master. But at this solemn moment, when he stood trembling, fearing his Lord would say, I will employ thee no more; thou art an unprofitable servant; begone from my presence!—yes, at this moment,—"one of the seraphim flew to him, having a coal in his hand, which he had taken with the tongs from off the altar; and he laid it upon his mouth, and said, "Lo, this hath touched thy lips, and thy iniquity is taken away, and thy sin purged," or expiated.'

The altar for burnt-offerings in the temple, had on it a perpetual fire; a lamb bled on it, and was consumed each morning and evening. This sacrifice was an emblem, or type, of the Lord Jesus, who was the true " Lamb of God, who taketh away the sin of the world."* "Without the shedding of blood there was no remission;" and "the blood of bulls and of goats could not take away sin;" it was of no avail for this purpose. These were but "shadows of good things to come, of which Christ was the substance."

Through the merit of the Saviour's offering, the Lord now assured the prophet that he was accepted in the Beloved; and that all his sins were pardoned. Now, he heard the voice of the Lord himself saying, " Whom shall I send; and who will go for us?" And the prophet could not help replying, "Here am I; send me!"

A sight of the grandeur and holiness of his Lord, and of his own sinfulness, struck him dumb; but a sense of God's pardoning mercy, opened his lips, and made him " ready for every good word and work."

A sense of God's pardoning love fills the soul

with holy joy. " O Lord," says the pardoned rebel, " I will praise thee, for though thou wast angry with me, thine anger is turned away, and thou confortest me."[7]

A sense of God's pardoning mercy fills the spirit with holy love. " I count," says the redeemed sinner, " all things but loss for the excellency of the knowledge of Christ."[7]

A sense of God's pardoning love will sustain the mind, and fill it with holy delight, in the midst of heavy affliction. " I reckon," says such an one, " that the sufferings of the present time are not worthy to be compared with the glory that shall be revealed in us."[7]

A sense of God's pardoning mercy will inspire the heart with holy zeal for the Divine honour. " I am ready," said one who enjoyed this great blessing, " not only to be bound, but to die at Jerusalem, for the name of the Lord Jesus."[7] Such persons have ever been the best messengers of the Lord to guilty men. They love him so much, that they regard the hardest task as easy, and the heaviest burden as light. Supported by the grace and strength of their Lord, nothing will move them from the right way; each of them will exclaim,

> "I cannot willing be
> His bounty to conceal
> From others, who, like me,
> Their wants and miseries feel;
> I'll tell them of thy bounteous store,
> And try to send a thousand more." [8]

QUESTIONS.

1. How do the seraphim employ their wings?
2. What did they cry?
3. Of what is the whole earth full?
4. What did the prophet say when he saw the Lord?
5. What did the seraphim do and say?
6. Who was the true Lamb of God?
7. Mention some of the fruits of the pardoning love of God.
8. Repeat the lines at the close of the story.

P

STORY XXVIII.

—❉—

THE ENQUIRY OF PETER.

THERE once came a very rich young man to our Lord, to ask what he should do that he might "inherit eternal life."

Among other things, our Lord said to him, "Go, and sell that thou hast, and give to the poor, and thou shalt have treasure in heaven; and come, and follow me!"

Our Lord said this to try him; that it might be evident whether he most loved God, or the world more than the favour of God, or that eternal life which he came to seek; for when he heard the advice of our Lord, "he went away sorrowful, as he had large possessions."

Then Peter said, "Behold, we have forsaken

all, and followed thee ; what shall we have therefore ?" Yes, Matthew did give up his place at the
"receipt of custom ;" Peter, and others, had left
their boats, and nets, and their kindred, and had
come to follow Christ. They had but little to
give up, but they gave up their all ; and they
could do no more. And God requireth according
to " what a man hath, and not according to what
he hath not." If they had possessed more, they
would have left it at Christ's command. But their
Master had repaid them ; he had provided for
them all that they had needed. He will not be a
debtor to any man.

And would you be his disciple, you must not
take the world, its honours, gains, nor pleasures,
as your portion; you must part with your sins,
though dear as " a right hand, or a right eye ;"
you must abandon wicked friends ; and renounce
your own righteousness, and trust in that of the
Saviour alone, for salvation.¹ And do you do so ?
His first disciples did so ; and he told them he
would give them peculiar honours.

And are you saying, What shall we have, if we take up our cross and follow the Saviour? You are not forbidden to ask the question. Our Lord himself "looked at the joy that was set before him, when he endured the cross, and despised the shame.". Moses, when he bare reproach for Christ's sake, "had respect to the recompence of reward."

What shall you have? In the present life, a large reward. Thus, when any have parted with friends for Christ's sake, God has raised up for them better friends; and when they have lost their substance, God has conferred on them better treasures.' He is able to do for us more than we can ask or think. His are "the cattle upon a thousand hills."

And he has given, and he does give, what is better than houses, or lands, or any worldly good; for he gives them the privileges of his children; he admits them to intimate converse with him; he gives them "joys that are unspeakable, and full of glory;" he makes their path shine brighter and brighter, till the perfect, the immortal day, breaks on their delighted vision.[3]

And, at last, when life shall close, he will call them as his children to inherit honours, riches and pleasures, surpassing the power of language to describe; even a portion greater than that of the mightiest kings; more to be desired than even the whole world. In the happy land where they are to dwell, there is no sorrow,—it can never enter into that blessed abode; all tears are wiped away from off all faces; "the days of their mourning are ended," and the days of their joy are begun, and are never to close.[4]

There will be no sickness, nor opening grave, nor parting there,—for Death has never entered, nor can he ever enter into that happy world.[4]

There they will see the Saviour, and be like him; and mingle in blest society with the great, and good, and wise, of every people, and kindred, and nation.[4]

This rest, this glory, and this joy, and more than any tongue can tell, or heart conceive, remaineth for every one of the disciples of the Saviour. "This honour have all his saints." O Lord, I beseech thee, bestow it upon me!

~~~~~~~~~~~~~~~~~~

QUESTIONS.

1. What must you do if you would be Christ's disciple?
2. What reward does Christ give his servants sometimes even in the present world?
3. What shall they have hereafter?
4. What is included in their portion in the unseen world?

STORY XXIX.

THE SAVIOUR'S CHARGE.

Soon after our Lord arose from the dead, he sought his disciples, and told them, among many other things, whither he would have them go, and what he would have them do.

He charged them to go into all nations, and to "preach the Gospel to every creature." During the life of our Lord, he sent them only to the "lost sheep of the house of Israel." But the apostle Paul travelled from Jerusalem even to Illyricum, which was nearly two thousand miles, to proclaim these tidings of great joy."

He charged them to preach everywhere repentance and remission of sins in his name; that is, by his authority, and through his mediation."[1]

God has joined these blessings together; and wherever he gives the one, he bestows the other. We are assured, that Christ is "exalted to give repentance to Israel, and remission of sins." [3] And all who really desire and ask for these blessings, shall be sure to receive them.

But he especially told them to begin their preaching at Jerusalem. How surprising was this! One should have supposed that he would rather have said, Go to all the cities of Israel; go among the Gentiles; go anywhere, only see to it that you go not near Jerusalem.[4] They have killed the prophets one after another; they scoffed at my instructions and my miracles; and, at length, they cast me out, and crucified me.[4] They have showed no mercy to my servants, let them have judgment without mercy.[4] See to it, that you go not near Jerusalem![4]

Besides, it will be utterly in vain. Can you expect to be more successful than your Lord? You know how often "I would have gathered them, as a hen gathereth her chickens under her wings," but they would not come to me.[5] It is of no use, therefore, to spend your strength for nought, and lose your precious time; go not, I charge you, go not to Jerusalem!

They saw me raise Lazarus from the dead, they beheld me when I gave sight to the blind, and when I fed the multitudes on the mountains.[6] They know that I am arisen from the dead; their own guards have told them so, yet they refuse to acknowledge it, and have given " large money" to the soldiers to spread abroad what they know to be a dreadful falsehood; the people, and priests, and rulers, have rejected me as the Messiah,— go not, therefore, I charge you, go not to Jerusalem![6]

Such, no doubt, would have been the language of even some of the best of the Lord's servants. But " his thoughts are not as our thoughts, nor his ways a sour ways, but are as high above them, as the heavens are higher than the earth." Go, preach " repentance and remission of sins among all nations, beginning at Jerusalem."[7] This was

as if he had said, Go and assure that hard-hearted
and wicked race, that I am ready to pardon them;
that I will receive, bless, and save them; and give
them a place in my family on earth and in heaven;'
not only go to Jerusalem when you have been
everywhere else,—but go now, and begin your
great work in the temple, in the streets and houses,
and public places of Jerusalem!'

There were many reasons why their Master
would have them begin their labours at Jerusalem.
No doubt one of them was, that it might be
evident that his Gospel was true.' Had they
gone to all places but Jerusalem, their enemies
might have said, they dared not show themselves
in that city: our Lord, therefore, said, Begin
your ministry at Jerusalem.' Here are five hundred of you,—you see that I am arisen; go tell it
to Jerusalem, in the very face of my foes. If
they doubt your evidence, I give you power to
heal the sick in my name, and to speak to people
of every nation, in their own tongues, the wonderful works of God.' And they did so, and multi-

tudes believed their testimony, and became the disciples of the Lord Jesus.

" Beginning at Jerusalem,"—this charge, no doubt, was to display the riches of his grace.* Perhaps our Lord knew that there were many in that city, who, like Simeon, were " waiting for the consolation of Israel," and he wished that they should be comforted. And he knew that there were many of his foes who cried out, " Away with him! Crucify him!" who would be grieved at heart for their sins, and seek after salvation, and he sent his servants to assure them, that even they, if they desired it, should be pardoned and saved.* It was as if he had said, Even these most guilty people shall not have to say, that there is no hope for them. No; go, proclaim the riches of my grace, " beginning at Jerusalem."

And he is still the same; still he invites " the weary and heavy laden," and he promises to give them rest. Still he says, " Whosoever cometh to me, I will in nowise cast out." Lord, show me my sinfulness; give me to see the infinite danger to which I am exposed; help me to fly to thee as the only and all-sufficient Saviour; and give me grace to love and serve thee for ever.[10]   Amen.

~~~~~~~~~~~~~~~~

QUESTIONS.

1. How far did the apostle travel to preach the Gospel?
2. What did our Lord charge his disciples to do?
3. For what is Christ exalted?
4. What should we have supposed our Lord to have said respecting Jerusalem?
5. What would our Lord have done in reference to Jerusalem
6. On what grounds were the people at Jerusalem without excuse?
7. What did Christ really say about Jerusalem?
8. Mention some reasons why our Lord would have his disciples begin their labours at Jerusalem?
9. How would he have them prove the reality of what they affirmed?
10. What should every one say to the Lord Jesus?

STORY XXX.

—✳—

THE LAME MAN HEALED.

It has been supposed, that there was a warm friendship between Peter and John, as we find them with each other on many occasions. After our Lord ascended to heaven, we read of their going up together to the temple.

The temple was always open among the Jews; we should go up to the house of God as often as we can, and not make vain excuses for the neglect of the public worship.[1] We should also go up "together;" taking our kindred and friends with us. Nothing but sickness, or something that makes it quite impossible, should prevent our going.[1] And no time can be improper: Peter and John went to the temple to pray, at three o'clock in the afternoon.

They saw lying at the gate of the temple called the Beautiful, a poor man, forty years old, who had been a cripple from his birth; he could neither work nor walk; and so some of his relations or friends carried him out every day, and put him down there to ask alms of those who went to worship. If we cannot give eyes to the blind, or feet to the lame, we should do what we can for them.

And Peter and John saw the poor cripple; they did not turn their eyes another way, or hasten by, as some people would have done; but they stood still, and Peter said, " Look on us!" And the poor creature did so, for he thought they would give him money to buy him clothes or bread. It is a great mercy to have food or raiment without begging for them.[2]

Now they knew that he looked for money; but they were so poor, that they had not any to give him. So Peter said, " Silver and gold have I none; but such as I have give I thee; in the name of Jesus Christ of Nazareth, rise up and

walk!" That is, by his power and grace. " And
Peter took him by the right hand, and immediately
his feet and ancle bones received strength." This
was a boon far better than gold and silver, or any
worldly treasure.*

And now the poor cripple, " leaping up, stood,
and walked, and entered with them into the
temple, walking, and leaping, and praising God."*
He tried his new-given strength in every possible
way ; he did not know enough how to show his
joy. And even when he got into the temple, he
could not keep quiet, but he kept on walking, and
leaping, and praising God! And if he had not
praised God, the stones might well have broken
their silence and reproached him.

No one can tell, but he who has lost his health,
and the use of his limbs, the joy which the return
of these great blessings inspires.* But he who
knows a little of what the poor cripple felt when
he entered " the temple, walking, and leaping, and
praising God," O ask such an one, and he will tell
you, that the heavens, and the earth, and the vast

creation, in that great moment, were adorned with a lustre which he never saw on them before. Yes, he will tell you, that every heart-string thrilled with gratitude and joy.[6]

And all the people in the temple " saw him walking, and leaping, and praising God;" and they would have thought him scarcely sound in his mind; but they knew that this poor man was the cripple whom they had so often seen lying help-less at the Beautiful gate of the temple, asking alms; and they were filled with wonder at the miracle that had been wrought.[7]

And as Peter and John were going out of the temple, and had reached the grand porch which was called by the name of Solomon, the poor man who had been healed, stopped them there, and held them fast, and would not let them go. But why did he do so? We know not. Perhaps he was afraid that when they were gone he should be a cripple again.[8] Perhaps he wished to point them out to the people;[8] as if he had said,—and who can tell but he did say,—when he laid hold of

them, Here are my benefactors!⁸ These are the
friends who gave me, not silver or gold, but what
is unspeakably more precious, the use of my
limbs!⁸ Come, and see them! Come, and hear
them!⁸ And the people ran together eagerly,
and surrounded Peter and John, that they might
hear all about this wonderful affair.

And Peter told them, that it was not by their
own power, nor skill, nor goodness, that this poor
cripple was healed; but that it was by faith in the
name, and power, and grace of the Lord Jesus,
that he had been made whole.⁹

And still the power and grace of Christ are
mighty to heal the diseases of the mind. And all
need to experience his healing power. This great
Physician is now saying to thee, Wilt thou be
made whole?[10] Wilt thou part with thy sins, with
the world as thy portion, with thy self-righteous-
ness, and wilt thou come to me as thy Prophet,
Priest, and King?[10] And wilt thou follow me
through evil and through good report?[10] Then
thou shalt be mine; then I will pardon, justify,

Q

sanctify, and save thee, "with an everlasting salvation." [10]

Who can tell how many this great Physician
has made whole! The apostle saw a very large
company of them; "they were arrayed in white
robes, and they had palms in their hands." And
he said, "Whence came they?" And the answer
was, "These are they who came out of great
tribulation, and have washed their robes, and
made them white in the blood of the Lamb.
Therefore are they before the throne of God, and
serve him day and night in his temple. And the
Lamb who is in the midst of the throne shall feed
them, and shall lead them unto living fountains of
waters; and God shall wipe away all tears from
their eyes." [11]

QUESTIONS.

1. What should we all do?
2. What is a great mercy?
3. What is the value of the use of our limbs?
4. What did the poor cripple do when he gained the use of his limbs?
5. What can no one tell?
6. What will he who has regained his health tell you?
7. What did the people in the temple know?
8. Why did the poor man who was healed hold Peter and John?
9. What did Peter tell the people?
10. What is Christ now saying to every one?
11. Whence did the large company which the apostle John saw come? And what is their happy condition?

STORY XXXI.

---*---

THE GIFT OF TONGUES.

AFTER the Lord Jesus arose from the dead, he stayed with his disciples forty days, that they might all know that he had really risen from the dead. Before he left them, he said, that if they waited at Jerusalem for a short season, the Holy Spirit should be poured out on them from on high in a very wonderful manner. And this promise was fulfilled : it could not be otherwise; there can be no reason why the Saviour should deceive his servants.

It was at the feast of Pentecost, which was fifty days after the Passover, and was kept in remembrance of the giving of the law on Mount Sinai, when one hundred and twenty of our Lord's disciples were met together in one place for prayer and praise, that the Holy Spirit was given to them in the fulness of his gifts and graces. "And suddenly," in answer to their prayer, " there came a sound from heaven, as of a rushing mighty wind, and it filled all the house where they were sitting. And there appeared to them cloven tongues, like as of fire, and it sat on each of them."

These tongues of flame were sensible signs to confirm their faith. So God gave to Abraham, on the same account, the vision of a burning lamp passing between the sacrifice. So the fleece of Gideon was wet or dry, according to his wishes.

Divine influence is here compared to fire. As fire melts the hardest metals, so God's Spirit softens the hardest heart. As fire consumes the dross, and separates the precious from the vile, so the Holy Spirit purifies the mind. As fire imparts light, so the Holy Spirit gives not only light, but eyes to behold it, and he who receives of this Spirit can say, "One thing I know, whereas I was once blind, now I see!" And as fire imparts warmth, so the Holy Spirit sheds abroad in the heart the holy flame of love to God, to the Saviour, to his people, to his word, and to all his commandments.¹ Have I received the Holy Spirit?

The Spirit came as a " mighty wind;" for his operations are "mighty." By this "mighty wind," the dry bones which the prophet Ezekiel saw, lived, and were clothed with flesh, and " stood up an exceeding great army;" by it, the covetous man, like Zaccheus, becomes generous, and the profane, godly.' Though wicked men may ridicule, he who feels as he ought, when he sees this great sight, will admire and adore, and exclaim, " Here is the finger of God!"'

Both the gifts and the graces of the Holy Spirit, were given in a large measure to the disciples on the day of Pentecost: one of the gifts were very wonderful; for " they began to speak with other tongues, as the Spirit gave them utterance." This was a great miracle, that persons should, without any previous thought, speak languages which they had never learnt, and of which, indeed, they before knew nothing, with fluency and correctness. Perhaps there is no greater miracle recorded in Scripture. It was wrought to confirm the truth of the Gospel; just as if one hundred English people should meet in London, persons from every part of the world, and should begin, as soon as they met with them, to preach to them, in their different languages, about the wonderful works of God.' What a mighty miracle would this be! Such was that wrought on the day of Pentecost.

But how do we know that this miracle was really wrought? In the same way that we know any other fact.' How do we know that there ever was such a person as king Alfred?' From the testimony of those who saw and knew him, which has been handed down to us from one age to another.' This is the only way in which we can be assured of events that have taken place. And the testimony which supports the facts mentioned in the Sriptures is very much stronger than that which proves any other events on record in the annals of the world.'

We should be much more desirous of the graces of the Holy Spirit than of his gifts. There is reason to fear that some have possessed the gifts, and have perished at last; all who are the subjects of his graces, will reach the kingdom of God.[c] Lord, bestow on me these blessed graces, even that faith which worketh by love; that repentance which is unto life; that joy, consolation, and peace, which the world cannot give, and which none can take away.

Thus these Jews spoke to the people of various countries of Europe, Asia, and Africa, in at least fifteen different tongues, " the wonderful works of God."

And what were these? No doubt, all the great truths of our holy religion. The undertaking of the Lord Jesus to seek and to save them that were lost; his taking on him our nature, though he was " the brightness of the Father's glory, and the express image of his person;" his miracles and doctrines; his sufferings, death, resurrection, ascension into glory; and his second coming, to

" judge the world in righteousness ;" the eternal misery of the wicked, and the everlasting blessedness of the righteous. These are, truly, the great and " wonderful things of God!"[8]

How earnestly we should pray for grace to watch over our tongues, that we may speak nothing but what is true, in lesser as well as great things; and nothing but what will do good to men, and bring glory to God.[9] " A wholesome tongue," says the wise man, " is a tree of life." All around may gather from it wholesome and delicious fruit. King David said, " I will take heed to my ways, that I offend not with my tongue." [10] We should say and do so too. And no man can properly regulate his tongue without the aids of the Holy Spirit.[11] Let us earnestly and humbly ask God to bestow them on us.

" The tongue is a little member," says the apostle, " and boasteth great things; behold, how great a matter a little fire kindleth ! The tongue is a fire, a world of iniquity ; it defileth the whole body, and setteth on fire the course of nature, and is set on fire of hell. The tongue can no man tame; it is an unruly evil, full of deadly poison." But though "no man can tame it," God can by his Holy Spirit; and if we ask for his influence, it will be given us. We should be often doing so; for, "if any man seem to be religious, and bridleth not his tongue, but deceiveth his own heart, that man's religion is vain:"¹² James iii. 2, 5.

QUESTIONS.

1. In what respect does Divine influence resemble fire?
2. Why is Divine influence called "mighty?"
3. What will the good man say of Divine influence, though wicked men may ridicule it?
4. What did that miracle resemble?
5. How do we know this miracle was wrought?
6. Why should we chiefly desire the graces of the Holy Spirit?
7. What should we say to God on this subject?
8. What are the wonderful works of God?
9. What should we pray for, and speak?
10. What did king David say?
11. How may we regulate our speech!
12. What does the apostle James say of the tongue?

STORY XXXII.

—✳—

CORNELIUS.

PART I.

CORNELIUS was a Roman soldier, and was an officer over a band of one hundred men. Some of all ranks and professions have been found in the service of God. Though Cornelius was a soldier, he was "a devout man;" and his heart was engaged by the influence of God's grace, to love and serve him.

"He feared the Lord with all his house;" that is, he feared to offend, and was desirous, above all things, to please him; and all his family were of the same mind with himself.[1] He could say, as the Psalmist did, "Mine eyes shall be on the faithful of the land, that they may dwell with me."

This good man had a very feeling heart, and he gave alms to those who needed them. He also was very exact in waiting on God in private and family devotion.[1] All the servants of the Lord, obey the Lord's commands as well as call upon him.[2]

One day, when he was alone praying, about three o'clock in the afternoon, there came an angel into his chamber; his countenance was bright and beautiful, and his apparel glorious. "Are they not all ministering spirits sent forth to minister to those who are heirs of salvation?" They are. No doubt they delight to minister to all who love and serve the Lord Jesus.

He seems to have known all about this centurion; for he addressed him by name, and said, "Cornelius!" The happy spirits know, perhaps, more about us than we imagine. "We are a spectacle to God, to angels, and to men!"

And Cornelius was filled with holy awe, and he asked him why he came? And the angel said, "Thy prayers and thy alms are come up for a memorial before God." He was amazed at this great honour conferred upon him; that "the high and lofty One who inhabiteth eternity," who regards "the heavens as his throne, and the earth as his footstool," should deign to hear his poor prayers, to notice his alms, and to send an angel to him! Yea, he does more than this, for he himself comes to visit all who love and serve him.*

No doubt but that his alms were the fruits of his faith and love; and these are always pleasing to God. "He will not forget them," Heb. vi. 10. Writing to the church at Philippi, the apostle says, "I am full and abound, having received the things which were sent from you, an odour of a sweet smell, a sacrifice acceptable, well-pleasing to God," Philippians iv. 18.

And the angel directed him to send to Joppa, a town about forty-five miles from Cesarea, where Cornelius dwelt, for a person named Peter, who should preach the Gospel to him, and tell him what he ought to believe and do.

But why did he not tell him these things him-

self? It could not be because he did not know
them; for the angels announced the tidings of the
Saviour's birth to the shepherds, who were "keeping watch over their flocks by night;" they saw
him in the garden when the big drops of blood fell
from him to the ground; they rolled away the
stone from the door of his sepulchre, and were
witnesses of his resurrection; and they sang his
praises as he ascended to his throne in glory.
But the angel knew that Peter could preach the
Gospel to Cornelius better than himself. So he
told him, that he would find this messenger of
mercy at the house of a person named Simon, who
was a tanner, who lived by the sea-side. God
knows us altogether: "what manner of persons,
then, ought we to be in all holy conversation and
godliness?"

And Cornelius had a servant who was "a devout
soldier, and waited on him continually." This one
fact seems to show that he loved God. "We
know," says the apostle John, "that we have
passed from death unto life, because we love the

brethren."' And do we love good people because they love and serve God?

And Cornelius sent this " devout soldier" and another servant to tell Peter what had taken place, and to invite him to Cesarea. So he " made haste, and delayed not to keep God's commandments." And we should do so too. We should be wise to-day ; we know not what will be on the morrow.'

QUESTIONS.

1. Tell me the character of Cornelius, and of his household.
2. What do all God's servants do ?
3. To whom are we a spectacle ?
4. What does God himself deign to do ?
5. What did the apostle say to the church at Philippi ?
6. What did the angels know of the Saviour ?
7. How may we know that we have passed from death unto life ?
8. Why should we be wise to-day ?

STORY XXXIII.

—✳—

CORNELIUS.

PART II.

Our Lord devoted his ministry chiefly to " the lost sheep of the house of Israel ;" and his disciples did so likewise ; nor is it very likely they would have done otherwise, had not God expressly called on them to do so. This he did in a wonderful manner.

Peter had gone up about noon to the top of the house to pray ; and God presented to the eyes of his mind, a vision as of a large sheet coming down from heaven, full of all kinds of animals, clean and unclean. And a voice was heard, saying, " Arise, Peter, kill and eat." But Peter objected, because, as he said, he had never eaten of any animal forbidden by the law of Moses. But the voice replied, " What God hath cleansed, that call not thou common." And the vision was repeated three times ; this was to convince Peter that he should not refuse, when called by God's providence, to go and preach the Gospel to the Gentiles. For all who indeed receive the Gospel, " are one in Christ Jesus ;"[1] so that, in the Christian church, all common distinctions are done away ; there is neither Jew nor Greek, Barbarian nor Scythian, bond nor free, but Christ is all, and in all."[2]

Now, whilst Peter was thinking of this vision, as he did not perceive its full meaning, the men from Cornelius were standing at the gate, asking after him by name. And the Holy Spirit bade him go with them, as he had sent them.

And the men came into the house, and told Peter about their master and their whole errand; and the next morning Peter, and all of his brethren, went with them; so wonderfully did God order things in his good providence. We should

R

"acknowledge God in all our ways, and he will direct our paths."³

Cornelius, expecting every hour a visit from Peter, invited his kinsmen and friends to his house, that they, as well as himself, might receive the benefit of his instructions.   If we love our friends as we ought, we shall be concerned to bring them to the Lord Jesus.⁴   If we indeed possess the grace of God, we shall care for the welfare of the souls of our relatives, and of all around us.   When the Saviour paid Matthew a visit, he invited many to meet our Lord.   When the woman of Samaria had met with the Messiah, she went and invited the people of the town, and said, " Come, see a man who told me all things that ever I did."

As Peter was entering the house, Cornelius met him, fell at his feet, and would have given him Divine homage, but he would not suffer him; he said, " Stand up, I myself am also a man!"

Now both Peter and Cornelius gave an account of the vision they had each seen; and the latter added, " We are all here present before God, to

hear all things that are commanded thee of God."
It is a fine sight to behold a whole congregation,
or family, all waiting to hear what God will say to
them by his holy word.[5]

Then Peter spoke to them very solemnly, and
said, " Of a truth, I perceive that God is no
respecter of persons; but in every nation, he that
feareth him, and worketh righteousness, is accepted with him."[6]

And are we among these happy characters?
Are we truly sorry for our sins? Do we fear to
offend God? Do we rely on the merits of the
Lord Jesus for salvation? And do we love him,
and obey his commands?

And then Peter declared to them the Gospel.
He told them how God had pitied poor sinners,
and had sent his only Son, who " is Lord of all,"
to atone for their sins, and satisfy the claims of
Divine justice; and that Christ is " our peace,"
and our peace-maker.

He also told them of the ministry of the Saviour,
how constantly he went about doing good; and

how he has " left us an example, that we should follow his steps." And are we trying, in the strength of Divine grace, to do so?

And he gave them an account of his sufferings, death, and resurrection; and of his coming, the second time, to judge the world in righteousness.

He affirmed, that he, and his fellow apostles, were witnesses of these things; for they had been with their Lord and Master, and had seen him, and ate and drank with him, after he had arisen.

And whilst Peter was preaching, the Holy Ghost fell on all that heard the word. What a blessed congregation was this, in which there was not one who was not converted. Still the word of the Gospel, by the influence of God's Spirit, is " the power of God unto salvation, to every one that believeth." ' Let each make the inquiry, Has it been so to me?

Not only were all who were present converted, but they were enabled to speak with tongues, as the apostles were on the day of Pentecost. And they praised God for the " glad tidings," which

Peter had announced to them. " Then answered Peter, Can any man forbid water, that these should not be baptized, which have received the Holy Ghost, as well as we ? And he commanded them to be baptized in the name of the Lord :" Acts x. 46, 8.

QUESTIONS.

1. What are all who receive the Gospel ?

2. What distinctions are done away in the Christian church ?

3. What should we do ?

4. If we love our friends as we ought, what shall we do ?

5. What is a fine sight ?

6. What did Peter say ?

7. What is the word of the Gospel by the power of God's Spirit ?

STORY XXXIV.

—✻—

THE DEPARTURE OF PAUL.

THE apostle Paul suffered death at Rome, under the cruel reign of the Roman emperor Nero ; and, most likely, by his immediate command.[1] As he speaks of himself, as " Paul the aged," no doubt he was far advanced in life.

A little before he was beheaded, he wrote to Timothy, to tell him how things were with him, and to give him his last solemn charge.

It is very pleasing to know, that though he was about to leave the world in this painful way, yet his mind was not only happy, but full of joy.

In his letter to Timothy he said, " I am ready to be offered, and the time of my departure is at hand. I have fought a good fight, I have finished my course, I have kept the faith; henceforth there is laid up for me a crown of righteousness, which the Lord, the righteous judge, shall give me at that day; and not to me only, but also to all them that love his appearing."

But what did he mean by this language? He meant many things which are worth knowing. He meant, that the Christian is, in some respects like a soldier, for he has many foes to overcome.[3] The men of the world—that is, those who take up with present things as their portion, and think and live as if there were no God; these sometimes want to turn him, by their smiles and caresses, from the narrow way that " leadeth unto life;" and often they try to do so by their frowns. Now a good man, in the strength of God's grace, has to resist them both. Thus Moses did. He was not moved from his duty by the smiles of Pharaoh, nor by his threatenings.[4] " He feared not the wrath of the king; he endured as seeing him who is invisible.[4] He chose rather to suffer affliction with the people of God, than to enjoy the pleasures of sin, which are but for a season." Blessed choice!

Paul meant, that, by Divine grace, he had done as Moses did; that he had fought against what was evil in his own heart; and that he had resisted the temptations of the great enemy.

What are these? They are many. These are some of them—do not fear to sin against God; care not about his favour; think not of the welfare of your soul; religion will rob you of your pleasures; seek your own enjoyment on God's holy day; go with the gay multitude of the ungodly; think not about death, nor judgment, nor eternity; call not upon God for his mercy, it will be time enough when you come to die.[5] These are dreadful sentiments. But what multitudes are ruined by them! Paul had, by God's help, resisted them. "I have," said he, "fought the good fight!"

He compares the life of the Christian to the races which were common in Greece.[6] These required diligence. Lazy wishes would not gain

the prize for any man; the Christian must " strive
to enter in at the straight gate." Paul did so:
" I press forward," said he, " to the mark, for the
prize of my high calling of God, in Christ Jesus."'

In those races, it was of no use to set out well,
to run a little way, and then give up the contest.
So, in the Christian race, none but they who hold
on and out to the end will be saved.*

In those races, persons laid aside their long garments, and heavy weights, or they could have had
no hope of gaining the prize; so Christians must
lay aside every weight, and the sin which most
easily besets them, and run with patience the race
set before them, looking unto Jesus," for all needful strength and grace.' And Paul had done so.
" I have," said he to Timothy, " finished my
course!"

And he adds, " I have kept the faith:" that is,
I have faithfully loved and preached all its great
and glorious doctrines; " I have not shunned to
declare the whole counsel," or will, " of God."
And now his heart was full of holy delight, as he

thought of the prospect which was before him.
And what was it?

" There is laid up for me," he said, " a crown,"
—what, such as earthly kings wear?   No; but as
we are used to include all that mortals can wish,
in the possession of a crown, so the apostle means,
that he was going to enjoy all his utmost wishes
could desire.   The favour of God; his life-giving
presence; the society of his Redeemer, and that of
the blessed in glory; perfect holiness, and perfect
joy; and far more than all the words which men
have invented can describe; and all these blessings
are for ever and ever;[10] these, all these, are included in that " crown" which the apostle was
about to wear.

Many crowns which earthly kings and con-
querors have worn, have been procured by injus-
tice and cruelty; but this crown was a " crown of
righteousness;" not, indeed, gained by his own
goodness, but by the infinite merits of the Lord
Jesus."[11]

Thus he says it would be " given" him on the

day of his entrance into glory. Men may give to their fellow-men the riches, honours, and pleasures of the world, but they cannot bestow the smallest blessings in the world beyond the grave. But it is our heavenly " Father's good pleasure " to give us a glorious kingdom there, even a kingdom that " cannot be moved."

And it gave pleasure to Paul, when he was going to enjoy this crown of glory, that there were very many more, even " a multitude that no man can number," on whom the Lord Jesus will bestow this great blessing, even on all who have committed their souls into his hands, and who are looking, with hearts full of love to him, for " his second coming, without sin unto salvation."[12]

Paul was not glad, as some people seem to be, that there would be only a few people in heaven besides himself; but he rejoiced, when he was about to die, that there would be a great many there.[13]

And do I strive, let each ask himself, and pray, that my friends, and parents, and brothers, and sisters, may be all there; and, especially, that I may indeed reach that happy state? I am sure I ought to do so.

Soon after Paul wrote this delightful letter to Timothy, he suffered death; we don't know exactly how. Perhaps Nero sent one of his soldiers to behead him in prison, as Herod did John the Baptist; or, perhaps, he was murdered in a more public way; or, perhaps, he might have been burnt, as many others were, at night, by fires kindled to light up the gardens and pleasure grounds of the Roman emperor.[14] But it matters not how his spirit was separated from the clay tenement in which it only lodged for a season. We are sure it was well with him, and that, " absent from the body, he was present with the Lord."

If we were dying,—and this will soon be the case,—could we look back, as Paul did, with holy joy? Could we say, that we had fought the good fight, and run the Christian race, and that we had kept, that is, loved and rejoiced in the great truths of the blessed Gospel? Or must we be compelled to look back on a life prayerless, Christless, and ungodly? Let us examine.

For as our faith and life have been, such will be our prospects at that solemn moment of our departure. How earnestly should we pray, that they may be as glorious and delightful as those of the apostle!

How excellent is that religion of the heart, which thus enables a man to exult when he is leaving all which the world calls good and great; yea, even when the spirit is going into the immediate presence of God! surely, this, this is " the one thing needful!"

> " Let the proud witling argue all he can,
>   It is religion still that makes the man;
>   'Tis this, 'tis this, which makes our morning bright,
>   'Tis this which gilds the darkness of the night;
>   And when disease invades the lab'ring breath,
>   When the heart sickens, and each pulse is death;
>   Ev'n then religion shall sustain the just,
>   Grace his last moments, nor desert his dust." [15]

QUESTIONS.

1. Who put the apostle Paul to death?
2. What did Paul say of himself in his letter to Timothy?
3. What character is the Christian like?
4. What was the character of Moses?
5. Mention some of the temptations of the enemy.
6. To what does Paul compare the Christian life?
7. What did Paul do?
8. Who are they who alone will gain the prize in the Christian race?
9. How must Christians run their race?
10. What is included in the crown which the apostle expected to receive?
11. How did Paul gain this crown.
12. To whom will the Lord give this crown?
13. Of what was Paul glad?
14. How did Paul die?
15. Repeat the lines at the close.

FINIS.

G. BERGER, PRINTER, Holywell Street, Strand.

CPSIA information can be obtained
at www.ICGtesting.com
Printed in the USA
BVHW041911110821
614215BV00010B/309